The Lighthouses of Connecticut

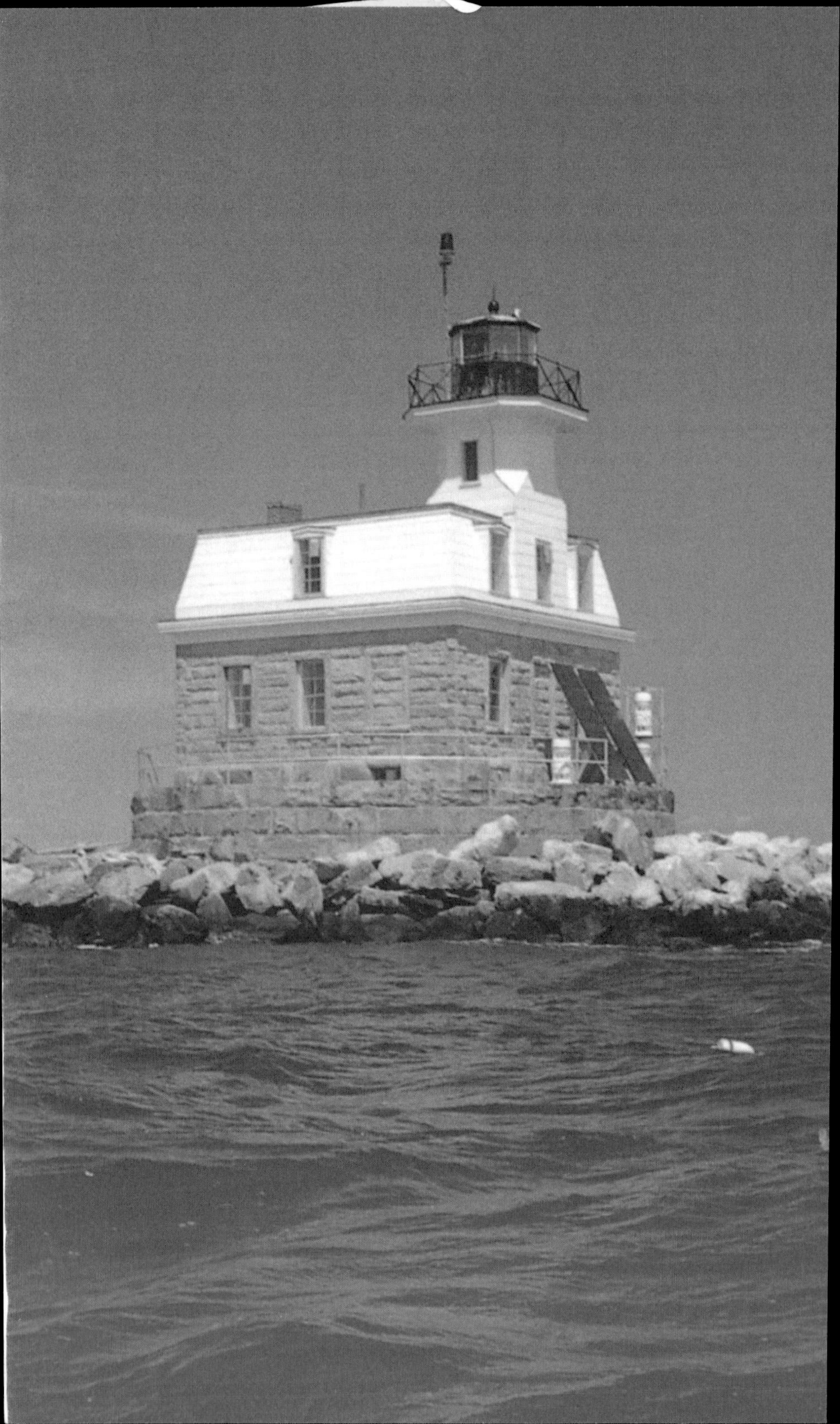

The Lighthouses of Connecticut

Jeremy D'Entremont

Commonwealth Editions
Beverly, Massachusetts

ISBN-13: 978-1-889833-70-5
ISBN-10: 1-889833-70-3

Library of Congress Cataloging-in-Publication Data
D'Entremont, Jeremy.
The lighthouses of Connecticut / Jeremy D'Entremont.
p. cm. — (The lighthouse treasury series)
Includes bibliographical references and index.
ISBN 1-889833-70-3
1. Lighthouses—Connecticut. 2. Lighthouses—Connecticut—History. I. Title.
VK1024.C8D46 2005
387.1'55'09746—dc22
2005005519

Cover and interior design by Stephen Bridges.
Layout by Anne Lenihan Rolland

Printed in the United States.

Commonwealth Editions
266 Cabot Street, Beverly, Massachusetts 01915
www.commonwealtheditions.com

Lighthouse Treasury Series

The large photo on the cover is of Five Mile Point Light. The small photos are, top to bottom, of Stratford Point Light, Avery Point Light, Black Rock Harbor Light, Lynde Point Light, Saybrook Breakwater Light, Faulkner's Island Light, and Morgan Point Light. The photo on the frontispiece is of Penfield Reef Light.

Contents

Preface

My main focus in these pages is on the people of the lighthouses, past and present. The buildings themselves are worthy of admiration and preservation, and I've tried to give lighthouse architecture, technology, and administration their just due. But it's the keepers and their families who brought these locations to life. There's a vivid cast of characters involved with the lighthouses of Connecticut, from Keeper Kate Moore, credited with twenty-one lives saved in more than six decades at Bridgeport's Fayerweather Island, to Theed "Crazy" Judson, keeper at Stratford Point, whose reported sightings included a sea serpent and a bevy of mermaids. There are also dark stories of madness and violence at some of the isolated offshore locations.

The human stories didn't end when the lights were automated and the keepers were removed. Preservationists have now become keepers. Communities, historical societies, and individuals have heeded the call to save our lighthouses as irreplaceable representatives of times past. The keepers of years past battled waves and wind, while today's preservationists fight red tape and funding shortages. But these struggles require no less stamina and determination. I've attempted to convey that here with some stories of recent lighthouse rescues, like the valiant work of the Avery Point Lighthouse Society, Faulkner's Light Brigade, the Norwalk Seaport Association, and others. These groups are making tomorrow's history as they strive to save the past.

The lighthouses discussed in this volume have been included in other books on the lighthouses of the northeast or New England, but are usually not focused on as a distinct group. Some of you might ask, "How can you write about these lights without including their close neighbors in New York territory?" A valid question for sure. There are New York lighthouses, especially in the vicinity of Fisher's Island, that are much closer to the Connecticut mainland than they are to Long Island. All the lights in this vicinity work together to aid mariners, and their pasts are intertwined. I apologize to anyone hoping to find lights like Latimer Reef, Little Gull, or Race Rock here. Although easily visible from Connecticut, they're officially in New York.

A decision was made as I embarked on this "Lighthouse Treasury" series with Commonwealth Editions that the lighthouses will be examined state by state. Volumes to follow this one in the next several years will cover, in order, Rhode Island, Massachusetts, Vermont and New Hampshire, and Maine. We may also venture outside the New England region in the years to come. The rationale for dividing the lighthouses this way is simply that you have to draw the line somewhere. Dividing the locations by state seems to be a tidy approach.

The brief final chapter here deals with "miscellaneous lights and lightships." The lightship buffs among you may feel that this vital part of maritime history has been given short shrift. The focus of this book is lighthouses and their keepers, but I didn't want to omit the subject from this book entirely. The history of lightships has been well told by other authors. The men who served on lightships were as dedicated and brave as any at lighthouses, and the vessels were a vital link in our system of navigational aids.

I wish to express my deep gratitude to the many organizations and individuals who provided invaluable help in the course of my research. I especially extend my thanks to the United States Coast Guard (the personnel both in New England and at the Coast Guard Historian's Office in Washington, D.C.), Connecticut State Library, National Archives, *Lighthouse Digest,* General Services Administration, Harbour Lights, University of Connecticut, Greenwich Chamber of Commerce, Historical Society of the Town of Greenwich, Greenwich Library, New-York Historical Society, Stamford Historical Society, Ferguson Library in Stamford, Norwalk Seaport Association, Norwalk Museum, Norwalk Historical Society, Norwalk Public Library, Fairfield Historical Society, Fairfield Public Library, Bridgeport Public Library Historical Collections, Barnum Museum, *Connecticut Post,* Stratford Historical Society, Stratford Library, Lighthouse Point Park (New Haven), New Haven Colony Historical Society, New Haven Free Public Library, Faulkner's Light Brigade, Old Saybrook Historical Society, New London Maritime Society, New London Ledge Lighthouse Foundation, Avery Point Lighthouse Society, Project Oceanology, Noank Historical Society, Mystic Seaport, Stonington Historical Society, Mystic and Noank Library, Old Lighthouse Museum in Stonington, American Lighthouse Foundation, and New England Lighthouse Lovers.

At the risk of omitting someone who's helped along the way, I want to single out the following individuals who went above and beyond when I asked for their help: Jason and Rena Pilalas, Margaret Bock, Joel Helander, Harold Petzolt, Carol Lovell, Lewis Knapp, Steven Young, Ed Skvorc, Terry McCool, Phil Vallie, Jim Streeter, Don Burr, Chief Petty Officer Michael Allen, Chief Warrant Officers David

Waldrip and Peter Boardman, Senior Chief Boatswain's Mate J. J. Nolda, Capt. Joseph Coccia, Dr. Robert Browning, Scott Price, Ron Foster, Michel Forand, Bob Trapani, Bob Shanley, Lois and Norm Valentine, Susan Gunn, Mary Witkowski, John Weigold IV, Jeffrey Spendelow, Brian Tague, David Barbour, Jim Claflin, Candace Clifford, Russ Rowlett, James Campbell, Louise Pittaway, Tim Harrison, Kathleen Finnegan, and Dee Leveille. Thanks also to all my friends and e-mail pals in the lighthouse world who have been so helpful and supportive as a matter of course for years. There are so many more I could mention. If you've helped me in the course of this research or any of my lighthouse projects, please know that you have my sincere appreciation.

I also offer thanks and praise to my wife, Charlotte Raczkowski, on whom I can always count for clear-eyed and incisive commentary on my work. And I thank my mother, Beatrice Meryman, for her ceaseless support.

Finally, a big thank-you to Commonwealth Editions, especially Webster Bull and editor Penny Stratton. Their professionalism, skill, and good humor have made it a rare pleasure to work with them on several projects. I feel genuinely lucky to be aligned with people who have a clear and enthusiastic understanding of all that's wonderful about New England and maritime history.

I hope you enjoy this first volume of the "Lighthouse Treasury" series. May the lights always burn brightly.

Jeremy D'Entremont
Portsmouth, New Hampshire
May 2005

Great Captain Island Light in 1999. *Photo by the author.*

Great Captain Island Light

1829, 1868

In July 1640 Robert Feake and Capt. Daniel Patrick of the New Haven Colony acquired a swath of land between the Asamuck and Patromuck Rivers, an area now known as Old Greenwich, from the local Indian sachems for "twentie-five coates." Patrick was killed in 1643 in a dispute with a Dutch soldier, but the "Great Captain" is remembered in the name of the 17-acre island a little over a mile from the shores of the town. Some people will tell you the island is named for a fabulous treasure buried by pirate Captain Kidd, but that seems to be a legend of recent origin.

Great Captain is the largest of a three-island archipelago. There's also Little Captain Island, today known primarily as Island Beach, with Wee Captain attached by a sandbar. According to Spencer P. Mead's 1911 *Ye Historie of Ye Town of Greenwich,* "Justus Bush . . . of Rye, N.Y., settled in Horseneck, now the Borough of Greenwich, about 1715, and later bought the islands from the estate of Dr. Nathaniel Worden. . . . Bush died in 1760 and left the islands to his children."

The only hitch was that New York also laid claim to the island, and letters of patent were granted to John Anderson of Oyster Bay. Things heated up when Anderson cut down trees on the island and the Bush family sued him for trespassing. The Superior Court of Fairfield County, Connecticut, found in favor of the plaintiffs—hardly a surprise! But then the legislature of New York passed an act in 1788 saying the island was part of Rye, New York. And so it went until 1880, when the dispute was definitively settled by a commission in favor of Connecticut.

Great Captain Island's position near the main shipping channel through Long Island Sound, as well as its proximity to other islands and dangerous ledges and shoals, made it an ideal place for a lighthouse to serve as both guide and warning. On March 3, 1829, Congress appropriated $5,000 for "a light house on Great Captain's Island, or Greenwich Point, or some other fit place . . . in Long Island Sound." Samuel Lyons sold three and a half acres on the southeast part of the island for $300 to the federal government to establish a light station. The land for the lighthouse also had to be ceded by the states of New York and Connecticut, since both still claimed ownership.

A 30-foot stone lighthouse was built for $3,455.17 by contractor Charles H. Smith, and it went into operation in 1829. It was one of seven major lights marking the main channel through the sound. The light also guided local traffic headed for the harbors of Greenwich, Stamford, and Cos Cob. Nine years after the light went into service, a report by Lt. George M. Bache of the U.S. Navy drew a bleak picture:

> *Its elevation is 62 feet and limit of visibility 14 miles; but it is barely discernible in clear weather at a distance of 9 miles. . . . The tower . . . is of rough stone, and is badly constructed; the mortar used in the masonry has not hardened, and the walls are cracked in several places.*
>
> *The lighting apparatus consists of ten lamps, with parabolic reflectors, arranged around two circular tables, and showing light in every direction. . . . The reflectors are 14½ inches in diameter . . . the silver is much worn from their concave surfaces. . . . The condensed moisture in the lantern occasionally freezes on the glass.*

Things hadn't improved much by 1850, when the following inspection report was made during George W. Anderson's tenure as keeper:

> *Light-house is leaky in the tower, and needs to be repointed and whitewashed. Dwelling is leaky about the windows, and I suppose always was. Lighting apparatus is miserable. . . . The whole of the establishment is in a neglected and filthy state. Lighting apparatus ought to be new, and there ought to be a new keeper, or the present one made to keep things in better order.*

A new lantern and a fourth-order Fresnel lens made by L. Sautter of Paris were installed in 1858. Finally, an appropriation of $12,000 was made on March 2, 1867, for a new lighthouse. The Lighthouse Board at that time decided on a standardized design for six Long Island Sound lighthouses: a sturdy granite dwelling with a cast-iron light tower (51 feet high in this instance) at the peak of the roof's front end. The other lighthouses with this design were Sheffield Island and Morgan Point, Connecticut; Old Field Point and Plum Island, New York; and Block Island North, Rhode Island. According to an article in the July 1987 Greenwich Historical Society *Newsletter*, the granite used at Great Captain Island was quarried in Greenwich.

The rest of the nineteenth century seems to have passed quietly on the island, with Civil War veteran Eliakim Worden serving as keeper from 1871 to 1890. The families in that era kept cows, chickens, and other animals at the station and also maintained a garden. It was reported that as many as 200 sail and steam vessels were seen from Great Captain Island at one time in 1890, but despite the heavy traffic there had been no wrecks in the vicinity since 1850.

A new fog signal building was added in 1890 with a steam-driven fog whistle and coal-fired boilers. A new foghorn with 13-horsepower oil engines in duplicate went into operation on June 10, 1905. Nine days later an article appeared in the *New York Herald* with the headline "Siren Is Breaking Up Happy Homes." "There were no nicer places to live in along the Sound until two weeks ago," wrote an inspired staffer. "But how may one dream if, just as the brain shapes some vision, there comes through the night a screech like an army of panthers, weird and prolonged, gradually lowering in note until after half a minute it becomes the roars of a thousand mad bulls, with intermediate voices suggesting the wail of a lost soul, the moan of the bottomless pit and the groan of a disabled elevator."

The writer claimed that locals were "organizing against the siren." The Annual Report of the Lighthouse Board for 1906 reported, "A fog-signal house was built, and various repairs were made." The "repairs" apparently included a dampening or repositioning of the horn, and area residents caught up on their rest.

A November 1904 article by Arthur Hewitt in a magazine called *The Outlook* described a visit of the lighthouse tender *Larkspur* to Great Captain Island, chiefly to deliver coal to run the fog signal. Eugene Mulligan had been keeper since 1890. Hewitt wrote:

> *I went ashore and chatted with the keeper. He showed me over his quarters and explained his light; everything was remarkably spick and span. His eyes, however, bore the look of a constant sufferer—eyes dulled by anguish and continued heartache. Wondering at this, I inquired how he liked the life; he replied, "It was all right while she was here, but now 'tain't any good any more."... When I inquired why, now that his life's partner was dead and gone, he did not ask for a transfer where scenes would at least be new and therefore brighter, he muttered something about not wishing to "bother" the inspector; he might as well keep the light, some one had to do it.*

Things didn't get much better for Keeper Mulligan. He had a series of run-ins with an assistant named Otto Rudolph. One day the two men quarreled over who would scrub the lighthouse steps. As the argument escalated, Mulligan dared Rudolph to strike him. The assistant proceeded to punch his superior in the face, blackening both of his eyes. Mulligan's sister was present and offered a wooden plank, suggesting that the keeper break it over Rudolph's head. He respectfully declined.

Keeper Mulligan filed a complaint with the local police. The authorities were faced with an unusual dilemma. If they tried Rudolph, they needed Mulligan on hand as a witness. But it was not permissible for both men to go ashore at the same time, since they'd be abandoning the light and foghorn. The *New York Times* reported, "Sheriff Ritch . . . has weak eyes from sitting up nights studying the question. And Sergt. 'Andy' Talbot, his assistant, is drooping from carrying law books back and forth between the Court House and the sheriff's home." The sheriff contemplated holding court on the island. But the lighthouse authorities discharged Rudolph, and the charges were dropped.

On rare occasions, large sections of Long Island Sound have frozen over. One resident reported having walked and ice-boated out as far as the lighthouse in the early 1900s, and even having seen an old Ford car that far out.

With much recreational boating in the area, the keepers were sometimes involved in rescues. In October 1929 Keeper Adam L. Kohlman was recognized for his rescue of two small boys from drowning. Kohlman was the stepgrandfather of Lois Valentine of Pennsylvania, who fondly remembers visits to the island in the 1930s and 1940s:

> *When school closed . . . they would come in and pick me up in the boat and I would stay all summer. There were always lots of visitors during the summer. My grandmother was glad for the company, but it proved to be a lot of work cooking large dinners to feed the gang.*
>
> *There was no telephone or electricity and all supplies and doctor visits were by the little boat. My grandparents had a large garden, which was very well tended, plus they raised chickens. The brass was polished and the paint always looked new, and the light was often inspected by the Lighthouse Service.*
>
> *My grandmother would often wake when a fog rolled in and turn on the foghorn without even waking my grandfather.*

Keeper Kohlman joined the Coast Guard after they took over the operation of lighthouses in 1939, and his wife had to live ashore. A few years later the Kohlmans were transferred to Throg's Neck in New York. Lois Valentine went to the island in 1993, her first visit since she was 13. She was amazed how much of the island near the lighthouse had eroded away and that the boardwalks were gone.

A 1949 article by Meyer Berger in the *New York Times* described life at Great Captain Island during the Coast Guard era. Four men were assigned to the station, and they barely left except for a six-day leave each month or an occasional grocery run. Winter was rough, but the summer months allowed the men to swim and fish.

The crew at the time included Chief Boatswain Mate John Bolger, a 22-year veteran and "devout man of middle age"; Ronald "Lucky" Lepre, a thin, black-haired 18-year-old from Los Angeles; Herb Gilchrist, a 20-year-old New York native; and John Lamb, a 26-year-old blond Texan. Keeping the men company was a black part-chow dog named Jerry, who loved barking her greetings to visitors from the high rocks.

Keeper Adam Kohlman cleans the Fresnel lens at Great Captain Island. *Courtesy of Lois Valentine.*

The Coast Guard crewmen joked about the solitude. "You slip so easy you don't really know you're going nuts," said Gilchrist. But the men hardly lived a monastic life with TV, radio, and a small gym.

Up until March 1968, the crewmen were still hand-cranking the clockwork mechanism that turned the revolving lens. Later the same year, the Coast Guard decided to replace the lighthouse with an automated light on a steel skeleton tower nearby. By this time there were only two men on duty at once, with two weeks on followed by a week off. James Honeycutt, one of the crewmen, told the *Greenwich Time* that he and the other men all cooked and cleaned, joking, "What we are is a bunch of housewives." The men played pool, lifted weights, and shot ducks and rats to pass the slow hours. The lighthouse was officially replaced by the new steel tower on January 30, 1970, and the Coast Guard crew was reassigned.

The rest of the island had been sold in 1926 to investors who planned to transform it into a "bungalow community." It was sold again three years later and the Great Captain's Island Corporation built a clubhouse and cabanas, but their high hopes for an exclusive resort were dashed by the Depression. After World War II the Port-Green Corporation transformed the old clubhouse into a casino.

On August 23, 1947, two army fliers died when their plane went into the sound. A Coast Guard plane dropped a flare during the search

U.S. Coast Guard photo from September 1935. *Photo by R. C. Smith.*

for the fliers. The flare landed on the casino and burned it down, ending another attempt to develop the island as a resort.

In 1955 the island, except for the light station, was bought by the Aerotech Company, which turned it into an employee vacation colony. In 1966 the town of Greenwich purchased 13 acres from Aerotech for $90,000. The town acquired the light station property from the Coast Guard in 1973.

After the Coast Guard left early in 1970, vandals almost immediately caused heavy damage to the lighthouse. Town officials realized a caretaker was a necessity, so they deputized Frederick Parnell as a special policeman and gave him the job. During their first summer on the island, Parnell and his wife lived in a temporary shack while the lighthouse was being readied. The situation was not appreciated by his wife, who told the *Greenwich Review*, "There's only so much crafts and needlework you can do." The Parnells were soon divorced, but Fred stayed on for a few years as caretaker.

Later, caretaker Robert Hendrix lived in the lighthouse with his wife, two dogs, four cats, four rabbits, and several tame squirrels. Hendrix improved the island's paths and kept the beach clean, and reported that bad weather sometimes kept him on the island for up to eight weeks straight.

More recently, Otto Lauersdorf spent over 15 years as the lighthouse caretaker. Originally from Germany, Lauersdorf was a U.S. Navy veteran and maintenance mechanic. His family spent some time on the island, but Lauersdorf was often alone. He went to town once a week to buy groceries and passed his days tending a garden, building model airplanes, reading boating and adventure books, and watching soccer and auto racing on TV.

A campaign to restore the lighthouse began in the late 1990s under the direction of the late E. Sidney Willis, longtime chairman of the Greenwich Chamber of Commerce. By early 2004 the Return the Light campaign of the Greenwich Chamber of Commerce's Let There Be Lights, Inc., had raised $250,000 for the return of the light to the lighthouse.

On September 7, 2003, a group of 80 people ventured out from Greenwich Harbor aboard the paddle-wheeler *Katinka.* Among the passengers were family and friends of those who died at New York's World Trade Center on September 11, 2001, and a memorial ceremony was held near the lighthouse.

Among the victims of the September 11 terrorist attacks was Greenwich resident Bennett Fisher, a senior vice president of Fiduciary Trust Company International. Fisher was one of the original forces behind the push to restore the lighthouse before his death, and much of the $250,000 raised was donated in his memory. Those involved in the lighthouse project plan to place a plaque on the building with the names of the 22 Greenwich citizens who died on September 11.

According to Mary Ann Morrison, president and CEO of the Greenwich Chamber of Commerce, the $250,000 will pay for lead abatement, paint for the exterior light tower, replacement of the glass in the lantern with Coast Guard–approved glass, a new tower venting system, an emergency backup navigation light, renovations of the interior and access to the tower, replacement of the roof flashing, and new wiring from the Coast Guard's solar power source to the lighthouse.

The town of Greenwich received a preliminary estimate of $850,000 for a total restoration, but the final cost is expected to top that figure.

Edward Bragg of Return the Light told the *Greenwich Time* why the September 11 memorial at the lighthouse is appropriate. "The lighthouse and the World Trade Center could see each other," he said. "It is a wonderful and fitting bond."

There's a public ferry to Great Captain Island in the summer, but it is available to Greenwich residents only. At present there are no public tours that pass the island.

Stamford Harbor Light in 2000. *Photo by the author.*

Stamford Harbor Light

(Chatham Rock Light, Ledge Obstruction Light)
1882

The city of Stamford traces its roots back to 1640, when Nathaniel Turner of the New Haven Colony paid the local natives with assorted trinkets and acquired a large area on the banks of the Rippowam River. The land was soon occupied by dissenters from the Church of Christ in Wethersfield. Agriculture long drove the local economy, but coastal and West Indies trade developed and the city became a major manufacturing center. Today Stamford is the fourth-largest city in Connecticut and the site of many corporate headquarters.

By the 1870s the sound waters near Stamford were bustling with steamers, barges, and schooners carrying a variety of goods from coal to oysters. According to the 1871 Annual Report of the Lighthouse Board, officials had visited Stamford, "in accordance with petition of a large number of persons interested in the trade of this port." They recommended both a day beacon and a lighted beacon at opposite ends of the channel. The cost of both, they said, would be $8,000.

Nothing happened for the next nine years, but on June 16, 1880, Congress finally appropriated $7,000 for a lighthouse. An additional $23,000 was appropriated the following March and Chatham Rock, about two-thirds of a mile from land, was chosen as the site. The state of Connecticut ceded jurisdiction over the site to the federal government, and plans were drawn for a cast-iron lighthouse atop a cylindrical cast-iron caisson. Engineer James Chatham Duane of the Lighthouse Board oversaw construction. Duane was the great-grandson of Judge James Duane, an early mayor of New York City. He was chief engineer of the Army of the Potomac during the Civil War and made important contributions to the construction of lighthouses, forts, and bridges.

Work on the lighthouse commenced in the summer of 1881. The Annual Report of the Lighthouse Board stated that "a temporary wharf was built at the site for the assembling of the iron, cement, sand, and other building materials, and for the facilities of sinking the sections of the pier." A shanty was erected on the pier, and foreman James Fagan and nine workers lived there during the construction. The caisson was set on cement laid on the ledge. Then the cylinder, 30 feet in diameter and 28 feet high, was filled with concrete and stones and surrounded by riprap (huge granite stones). A second, smaller cylinder was placed inside to serve as a basement.

The cast-iron superstructure was then added, 22 feet in diameter at its base and 15 feet at the top, topped by a 9-foot-high cast-iron lantern. The superstructure was 49 feet high. The lighthouse, painted with rust-resistant red lead, went into operation on February 10, 1882, with a fourth-order Fresnel lens replacing an earlier temporary light. A fog bell and striking machinery were also installed.

In its dimensions and design, Stamford Harbor Lighthouse is virtually identical to Latimer Reef Lighthouse, New York (1884), and Saybrook Breakwater Lighthouse, Connecticut (1886). The brick-lined basement contained a cistern for fresh water and space for oil storage. The first level of the lighthouse contained the kitchen and was surrounded by a gallery with a metal roof supported by stanchions. This gallery was rebuilt in 1927. The second (parlor), third (one bedroom), and fourth (two bedrooms) stories inside the tower served as living quarters for the keepers. Next came the watchroom and lantern levels, each with its own gallery. The bell-striking machinery was on the watchroom level.

The first keeper, Neil Martin, formerly at Race Rock Light, New York, served only until the end of October 1882. He was replaced by Civil War veteran Nahor (sometimes reported as "Naylor") Jones, who moved to the lighthouse with his wife, Julia. Jones built a new dock and brought a chicken coop to the lighthouse, but a northeaster destroyed the dock, coop, and chickens. According to a 1949 article in the *New York Times*, Keeper Jones commuted from Shippan Point in Stamford during the rest of his tenure. But he was apparently on duty at the lighthouse on July 9, 1884, when the excursion boat *Crystal Wave*, filled with passengers, went aground on High Water Rock about a quarter mile north of the station. Jones reached the vessel and piloted it safely to Shippan Point.

Adolph Obman served two stints as keeper, from 1904 to 1907 and 1909 to 1911. Toward the end of their stay, Obman and his wife, Frieda, welcomed a daughter, Elizabeth, who was born in the lighthouse on February 26, 1911. In a 1991 article, local resident William Muchinsky recalled that the Obmans had six children, all born in lighthouses from New Jersey to Rhode Island. Elizabeth was the youngest and the only one born in Stamford.

John J. Cook was the keeper between Obman's two terms. Cook, originally from Denmark, went to sea early in life and was said to possess a number of medals from his years in the U.S. Navy. In May 1908 a newspaper story with the headline "Heroine Passes Night of Terror" told a genuinely harrowing tale. Cook's mother-in-law, Louisa Weickman, was living at the lighthouse with her daughter Martha and Keeper Cook that spring. Martha was feeling ill and left to spend some time onshore with friends. After some days had passed, word came back to the lighthouse that she was anxious to return and Cook set out in the station's 15-foot motor launch to get her.

Cook picked up his wife and headed back for the lighthouse in the afternoon. The wind picked up from the northwest, and at about 5:30 Mrs. Weickman saw the boat approaching. Cook was struggling against the wind and tide and the boat was briefly hung up on a rock. The keeper got out in knee-high water and shoved the boat off, but another landing attempt was unsuccessful. Pushing off from another rock, Cook lost one of his two oars in the water. "We'll go back to shore and come out when this is over," shouted the keeper to his mother-in-law. "You keep the light going."

Mrs. Weickman watched the little boat drift away, but then a steamer passed by and she lost sight of the launch. She feared that they had been struck and killed by the steamer. "I have known a lot of sorrow," she said, "but I don't think I ever suffered so much as that night. I was powerless to do anything. . . . All I could do was watch, pray and hope." Despite her anxiety, Mrs. Weickman lit the lighthouse lamp at sunset and sat by one of the tower's windows. She stayed at the window all night. "Sleep I did not dream of," she said, "food I did not want."

The next day passed with no word. Finally, about 10:00 that night, a man came near the lighthouse in a boat and told Mrs. Weickman that Martha and John had been picked up on Long Island. They had gone ashore near Eaton's Neck, and a surfman from the lifesaving station there found the empty boat and then Keeper Cook plodding down the beach carrying his weakened wife in his arms. Cook was concerned that the light might have gone out in the lighthouse. But the lifesaving station crew contacted someone in Stamford and learned that the light had not failed. The family was soon reunited. "My prayers are answered," said Mrs. Weickman.

The following December, John J. Cook and family again made the newspapers. A reporter asked the keeper how he could possibly enjoy Christmas in such an isolated, lonely place. Cook's reply showed him to be quite a philosopher:

> *I dunno, it is pretty lonesome here sometimes, especially in winter, but we manage to enjoy our holidays. We can't go to church on*

Christmas and we miss the nice music and the fine sermons, but there is a compensation for that. What more soul-stirring music could there be than that of wind and wave as they whistle and roar or moan and swish past our little home?

And that light aloft is a sermon in itself. Many a fervent "Thank God," many a heart-deep prayer has gone up, maybe from people who wouldn't be thinking of such things ashore, when the red gleam of Stamford Light was made out in a storm, or the bell heard in a fog. My little light has its mission just as your pulpit preacher has his; and no one who has watched it through the terrible winter storms can fail to appreciate this, and with it his responsibility. Human life, yes, human souls depend upon that light Christmas and every other night of the year, and I dare guess it's compensation for the loss of a Christmas sermon to keep the light burning steadily.

Keeper Cook explained that with such unpredictable weather and sea conditions, preparations and Christmas shopping had to be done well in advance. He described the Christmas feast they had a year earlier, with goose, mince pie, and plum pudding. Christmas evening would be spent much like any other, with conversation, card playing, or perhaps reading books or newspapers.

It was not uncommon in winter for ice to pile up around the lighthouse, but the harbor rarely froze solid. But in the last week of December 1917, with the area already facing wartime coal shortages, a prolonged cold snap froze Long Island Sound from Connecticut to New York. The *Stamford Advocate* reported, "Motoring to the lighthouse is the latest winter sport." *Advocate* columnist Don Russell wrote in 1998 that when the harbor froze, people drove their Model Ts out from Jefferson Street onto the harbor and around the lighthouse, racing them back to shore.

Edward Iten was keeper for a few years in the 1920s. His daughter, Florence, later recalled that she never learned to swim, but would play on nearby buoys with her brother, Charles. According to her granddaughters Dawn Misawic and Deborah Messina-Kleinman, Florence also remembered a time near Christmas when her father climbed the ladder on the side of the lighthouse while playing Santa. Startled by his children, who looked out to see who was coming up the ladder, Keeper Iten dropped his sack of gifts into the harbor. Florence's tin wind-up toys were a bit rusty that year.

Iten also had a 25-year-old stepdaughter named Hazel, who in late 1926 married Greenwich native Rocco Roina. According to some, after the wedding Hazel had second thoughts about going ashore to live

An icebound Stamford Harbor Light in the early 1900s.
From the author's collection.

with her husband, wanting instead to stay with her family at the lighthouse. According to local resident William Muchinsky in a 1991 article, the groom finally convinced his bride to come ashore at Southfield Point, then promptly shot and killed her. A small item in the *Bridgeport Telegram* of January 24, 1927, reported that Roina then shot and killed himself.

Wrecks and incidents involving vessels of all sizes were not uncommon near the lighthouse. In November 1908 a barge being towed by the steam canal boat *J. C. Austin* struck a rock about 150 yards northeast by east of the lighthouse and sank. There were no injuries and the barge was refloated.

In 1929 it was reported in the *Lighthouse Service Bulletin* that "Edward M. Whitford, keeper, Stamford Harbor Light Station, Connecticut, on July 4 rescued three men, a boy, and a dog from a motor boat, which had become disabled in the vicinity of the station."

Raymond Bliven, a Rhode Island native who had been an assistant keeper at Stratford Shoal Light, came to Stamford as keeper in 1930. Described as a large and powerful man over six feet tall and close to 200 pounds, Bliven lived alone at the lighthouse, reportedly having separated from his wife. On the evening of Wednesday, August 12, 1931, after lighting the lighthouse lamp at sunset, Bliven set out in the station's boat to visit a friend named Charles Ford in Old Greenwich. The boat had an outboard motor, but on this occasion Bliven chose to leave the motor behind and row ashore. His last entry in the lighthouse logbook was at 3:30 that afternoon.

Bliven met with Ford to discuss an expected visit from Richard White, keeper at New York's Execution Rocks Light. The two men talked until about 10:30, when Bliven left to return to the lighthouse. Exactly what happened after that remains a mystery. A woman who lived in Old Greenwich with a view of the lighthouse called local police two nights later to tell them the light was out, and the police asked harbormaster Clarence Muzzio and his brother Emil to investigate. They found the lighthouse deserted, the lamp's oil nearly consumed, and the wick almost burned away. The two men refilled the tank with kerosene and got the light operating again. Meanwhile, the lighthouse tender *Spruce* arrived in the wee hours of Saturday morning.

The keeper's boat was soon found by the Muzzio brothers, floating upside down against some rocks about a mile north of the lighthouse. About 5:30 that Saturday afternoon Alfred Phillips Jr., a former mayor of Stamford, was in his yacht in Long Island Sound when he discovered Bliven's body floating about a half mile southeast of the lighthouse. He notified Capt. Victor Klang of the *Spruce* and the body was taken ashore.

1935 U.S. Coast Guard photo of Stamford Harbor Light. *Photo by R. C. Smith.*

Medical examiner Ralph W. Crane proposed the theory that Bliven had made it back to the lighthouse. While climbing the ladder, Crane believed, Bliven fell back onto the boat, turning it over. The doctor believed that the stunned or unconscious keeper then drowned. This theory was supported by the fact that three rungs of the iron ladder had previously been broken and replaced by wooden pieces lashed with rope—thus climbing the ladder was risky, especially at night. Another theory was that Bliven's boat was hung up on a rock and that when he tried to free it with an oar, he overturned the boat and was thrown into the water.

The 34-year-old Bliven was in good health, was a

good swimmer, and was not intoxicated at the time of his death. The body had bad cuts over the eyes, and the face and neck were discolored, raising the suspicion of foul play, but the death was ruled an accidental drowning.

Martin Luther Sowle became keeper in 1938. As it turned out, he would be the last official keeper of the lighthouse, staying until 1953. Sowle went out in the lighthouse's motor skiff on October 2, 1939, to rescue a man about two miles away, later receiving a Congressional Silver Medal for his heroism.

There were some rough times at the lighthouse earlier that same year, judging by entries in the station's log. In August, Sowle was onshore when Assistant Keeper Andrew A. McLintock wrote, "Temporary ass't keeper refuses to work. . . . After having cleaned up the mess he made in the hall . . . and washing the kitchen floor, I fixed a pail with a little water in it and told him there was another little job down stairs while he was in the kitchen, and received abusive language as the answer." The temporary assistant keeper, J. Marsden, subsequently entered in the log, "Left Stat. to get Keeper."

Peter Davenport of the *Stamford Advocate* wrote about this in a July 2004 column and noted that Marsden's entry looked shaky and that it looked like drops of liquid had dropped onto the page. "Are they beads of sweat dripping from his brow?" wrote Davenport. "Or are they tears?"

Under the Coast Guard, which took over the operation of the nation's lighthouses from the Lighthouse Service in 1939, Stamford Harbor Light had a complement of three men. Part of the old quarters was taken up by an engine room.

In 1949 the Coast Guard proposed discontinuing Stamford Harbor Light and replacing it with a modern automated light on the harbor's west breakwater. A public hearing was held on the matter in Stamford's city courtroom.

One of those opposed to the change was harbormaster John J. Ryle Jr. Ryle's father had also been harbormaster and captained the schooner that brought the stone that was placed around the lighthouse when it was first built. Local officials, representatives of local yacht clubs, and others joined Ryle in his protest. The objections bought the lighthouse a stay of execution.

In 1952 the Coast Guard again proposed to retire the lighthouse. Catherine Frewen Barlow of Old Greenwich wrote a letter to President Truman, saying, "Native Sons and Daughters do not look upon it as something made of stone and steel—but rather as a friend. They have a deep sentimental regard for Stamford Lighthouse." She claimed that many rescues performed by the keepers never made the newspapers and concluded, "The Lighthouse—Faithful Sentinel through the night casting its friendly beam of light over the waters of Long Island Sound. Save this grand old guardian of the Mariners from destruction!"

Ms. Barlow's letter was forwarded to Under Secretary of the Treasury G. H. Foley, who replied, "The sentimental regard for Stamford Harbor Lighthouse by native sons and daughters in the area is readily understood. However, at the same time one cannot overlook the fact that the Coast Guard is not authorized by law to preserve an aid to navigation for its local or historic interest value." He suggested that a local group might be willing to take over the lighthouse and explained that the decision to discontinue the light was "the result of careful study and deliberation of a Coast Guard Board constituted by direction of the President."

An official announcement was made in May 1953 that the light would be discontinued and replaced by a light and foghorn on the west breakwater. But the pleas of local residents were heard, and in mid-June it was announced that a flashing green light, operated from shore, would be retained at the lighthouse along with a foghorn. Willard Riley of Stamford was hired to be the "lamplighter" after the Coast Guard crew was reassigned in late June. Marty Sowle, the last keeper, spent some of his final days fishing at his favorite spot on the nearby breakwater.

By November 1953 the lighthouse was transferred to the General Services Administration (GSA) and put up for sale. In January 1954 the *New York Times* reported that a "band of hardy souls" was taken out to inspect the lighthouse "with a view to buying it, for reasons known only to themselves." One Greenwich woman said her husband made the trip with her consent. "It's an odd item that we could fix up for ourselves," she said. "Personally, I think it would be fun." Women on the tour reportedly measured the windows for curtains while men figured out where they'd put the bar.

The high bidder was Marvin Thompson, a Stamford pharmaceutical manufacturer. But Stamford Mayor Thomas F. J. Quigley started machinations to obtain the lighthouse for the city, saying it could be converted into a museum, weather observatory, or civil defense post. The state of Connecticut deeded the Chatham Rock site to the city of Stamford in May 1955, but it took until June 1956 before the federal government turned over the lighthouse to the city.

Despite the best of initial intentions, the city government provided only minimal maintenance and allowed the lighthouse to fall further into disrepair. In 1964 the structure was transferred back to federal control by quitclaim deed. A Stamford official urged quick action "before they change their minds," and the lighthouse went to the Department of the Interior. In July 1967 bids were once again taken for the lighthouse, and would-be buyers were told they could inspect the tower at their own risk. The *Stamford Advocate* jokingly referred to it as a "light elephant."

This time a partnership of three men submitted the high bid of $10,100. The men were Benjamin Gilbert, the commodore of the Stamford Yacht Club, and William Schwartz and Robert Loomis, who were local developers. Their plans were rather vague, as reported in a story with the headline, "Group Buys Lighthouse Without Knowing Why." By July 1969 the lighthouse was described by members of a scuba diving club as being in complete disrepair.

The lighthouse eventually reverted to the GSA again and was later sold to the Hartford Electric Light Company. When that company went out of business the property went to Northeast Utilities. They sold it at auction in 1984 and Eryk Spektor, a New York bank executive originally from Poland, purchased it for $230,000. His reason was simple. "I wanted to have a lighthouse," he told a local reporter. "It will be a cheap place to park my boat."

In June 1985 a crew hired by Spektor arrived to clean and repair the lighthouse. Paul Pugliese, a Greenwich architect, oversaw the project. By the time he was through with the renovation, Spektor had spent over $300,000. But as it turned out, Spektor spent little time at the tower and never even spent a night there, largely because his wife had no interest in boating or visiting the lighthouse. He hired John Weigold, who had bid against him when the lighthouse was sold, to manage the property. Weigold had helped with the renovation, including the removal of huge amounts of guano in the tower.

Weigold and Spektor announced at one point that they would rent the lighthouse out for weekends in summer. That never came to pass, and in 1997 the lighthouse was for sale at an asking price of $1.1 million. "YOUR OWN PARADISE—20 MINUTES TO SHORE!" read the real estate ad.

Eryk Spektor died in late 1998 and the lighthouse was pulled off the market. It again has gradually fallen into disrepair, but a light on top of the lantern (flashing white every four seconds) still serves as a privately maintained aid to navigation.

Stamford Harbor Light can be seen from the Shippan Point area, but the best views are by private boat.

CHAPTER 3

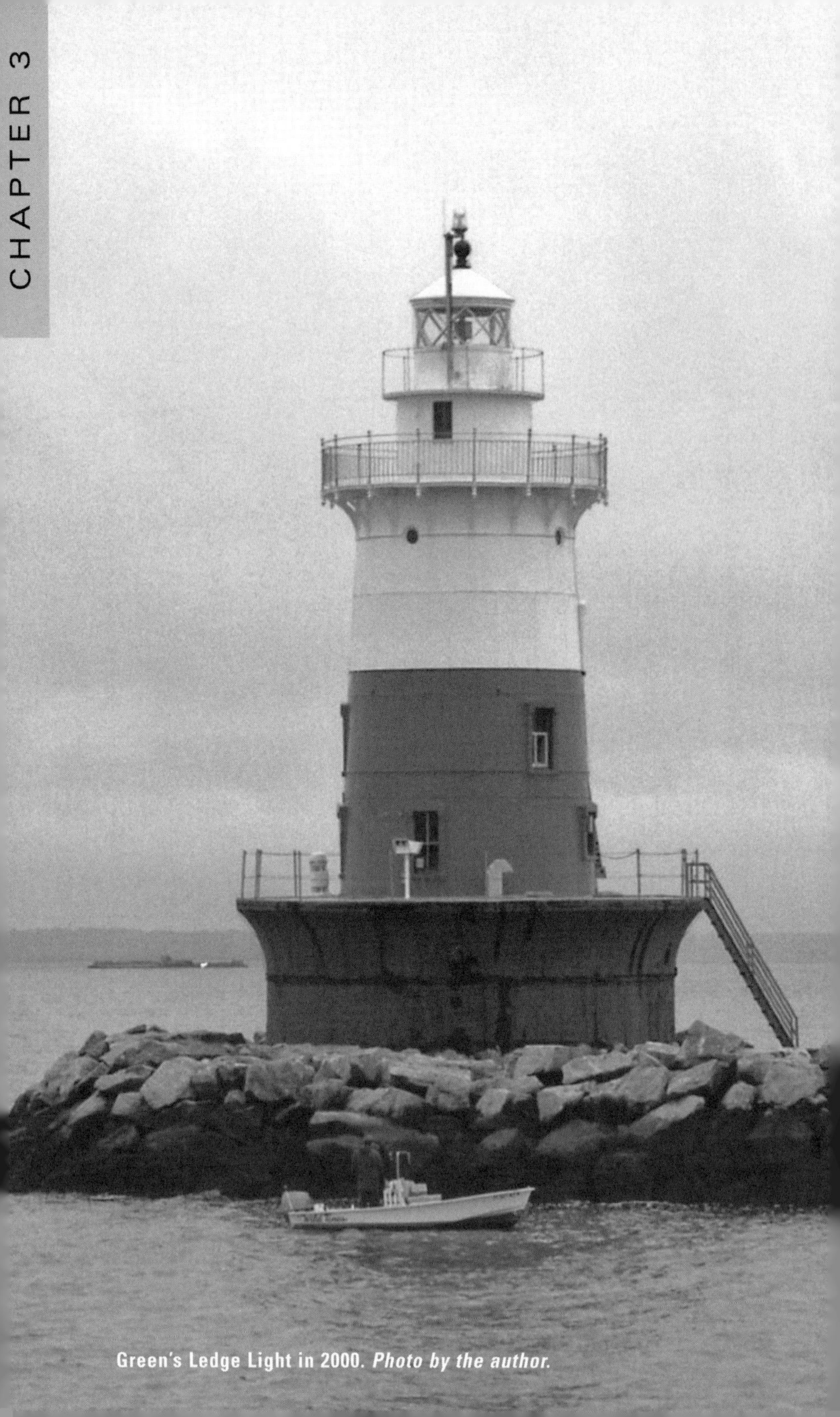

Green's Ledge Light in 2000. *Photo by the author.*

3

Green's Ledge Light

(Green's Reef Light)
1902

The name of Green's Ledge apparently has its roots in a local legend. According to journalist Dominic Mariani, quoted in Michael J. Rhein's book *Anatomy of the Lighthouse*, it was reputedly named for a pirate named Green who sailed with Captain Kidd. Folklore tells us that after Green was caught and executed, his body was displayed in chains on the ledge as a warning to would-be buccaneers.

The city of Norwalk bounced back from a disastrous raid in the American Revolution to grow into a major center for coastal trade, shipbuilding, manufacturing, and commercial shellfishing. For about three-quarters of a century beginning in 1826, the lighthouse on Sheffield Island served as the lone guide for navigating past the islands, ledges, and shoals on the approach to Norwalk Harbor at the lower reach of the Norwalk River.

In the late nineteenth century there was a push to improve the harbor and its approaches to accommodate more traffic and larger vessels. It was decided that navigational interests would be best served by the addition of a lighthouse on Green's Ledge at the western end of a treacherous shoal extending westward from Sheffield Island. The 1896 Annual Report of the Lighthouse Board called for an appropriation:

> *The proposed improvements to the aids to navigation in this harbor are rendered necessary by the important commercial interests of this port and the progress with works of harbor and channel improvement in this vicinity which are being prosecuted by the Government. It is proposed, therefore, to establish a light and fog-signal station on Greens Ledge, Norwalk Harbor, which is estimated will cost $60,000.*

After the request for $60,000 was made for a third straight year, on March 3, 1899, Congress appropriated the funds, and the site was subsequently surveyed. Plans and specifications for a cast-iron lighthouse atop a cylindrical cast-iron caisson were prepared. Work soon commenced and by January 30, 1901—a surprising time of year to be working on such a project in Long Island Sound—five sections of the caisson were in place and filled with concrete. The lower courses of the

An early 1900s postcard of Green's Ledge Light. *From the author's collection.*

caisson had been assembled on a wharf at Wilson's Point before being brought to the site.

The entire cylindrical foundation was finished by July 24, with the caisson reaching a height of 25 feet 5 inches. The cast-iron superstructure, including living quarters for keepers, was added during the rest of that summer and fall. By the end of October the structure was finished up to the floor of the watchroom.

Early in 1902, 1,500 tons of giant granite stones (riprap) were placed around the base of the lighthouse for extra protection from ice and storms. Duplicate fog signals were installed, run by 5-horsepower oil engines. A temporary fifth-order lens was in use by February 15, and by May a fourth-order lens was put into operation, with a white light interrupted by red flashes every 15 seconds. Meanwhile, the old light on Sheffield Island was discontinued. For about a dozen years the 1868 building was used as auxiliary space for the keepers at Green's Ledge.

The first-floor gallery of the tower originally had ornate cast-iron stanchions topped by a circular roof. The 52-foot tower has four stories, plus the watchroom and lantern. The first floor once contained the kitchen. The second, third, and fourth floors provided bedrooms and living space for the keepers. The second story also had a privy, an early example of an indoor bathroom on an offshore lighthouse. The entire tower was lined with brick up to the watchroom level.

Green's Ledge Light was always a "stag" station, with only male keepers and no families. The first keeper was William DeLuce, who stayed until 1908. His assistant until 1904 was Henry M. Bevedret. Few keepers or assistants lasted longer than a couple of years at the offshore lighthouse, which definitely was not considered a plum assignment.

John Kiarskon, a native of Sweden, arrived as assistant keeper in 1909 and was soon promoted to principal keeper. Kiarskon was to be a central figure in one of the most bizarre sequences of events in New England lighthouse history.

On March 2, 1910, Keeper Kiarskon left the lighthouse on the station's only boat, telling Assistant Keeper Leroy C. Loughborough that he was going to Norwalk to pick up provisions and both men's paychecks. He never returned. Eleven days later, the lighthouse tender *Pansy* landed at Green's Ledge and found Loughborough "half-starved, exhausted and almost crazy," according to an article in the *Washington Post.* Loughborough told authorities that during the time he was abandoned he lived on potatoes and dog biscuits, with only boiled salt water to drink.

Through the whole nightmarish ordeal Loughborough struggled to keep the light going along with the two engines for the fog signal. For three days he neither ate nor slept. During one 72-hour stretch there was continuous fog, and one of the engines failed. He struggled vainly to repair the engine, and meanwhile the light burned itself out. When the tender crew arrived to investigate the extinguished light, the assistant keeper was found, almost unconscious and with his dog at his side, on the floor by the engine. Loughborough later said that he would have shared his last biscuit with the dog.

It turned out that Kiarskon had gone to a local hotel, where he cashed Loughborough's paycheck for $44.69 and went on a drinking binge. He eventually gave himself up to Bridgeport police and was taken to South Norwalk. Kiarskon was immediately discharged as keeper and was expected to serve time in prison for forgery, but his ultimate fate is unclear.

"I feel ten years older and my hair has grown gray," said Loughborough after being taken ashore. He continued:

> *I would not go through that experience again for the United States mint. Several times I inverted the flag on the mast, intending to attract the attention of some passing boat and thereby escaping to the mainland, but the greater part of the time it was so stormy or foggy the signal could not be seen. Each time I would take it down, determined to stick it out to the end. I was almost out of my head from the strain. It would not have been so bad save for the awful fog, which made me keep at the engines night and day. It is well that the* Pansy *came when she did. I don't think I would ever have moved from that rug.*

Assistant Superintendent John S. Hayward was on the *Pansy* when Loughborough was found. On examining the lighthouse log, Hayward saw that Kiarskon had made no entries for 11 days, supporting Loughborough's story. The assistant keeper received high praise for his heroism in the face of abandonment and possible starvation.

Loughborough never recovered from the ordeal. A little less than a year later, in February 1911, he died of tuberculosis at the home of his father in Point Judith, Rhode Island. He was just 27 years old. Incredibly, this was merely the close of the first act in this particular drama.

William T. Locke was the next head keeper at Green's Ledge, and Leroy Loughborough's brother George became his assistant. One day in March of 1912 George Loughborough went ashore to South Norwalk. It was reported that while there he learned of an aunt's illness and went to visit her in Wakefield, Rhode Island. After 16 days, Keeper Locke was found alone at the lighthouse, weak and exhausted. He told the authorities that he had gotten little sleep since the assistant left, and had reduced his daily rations to a minimum out of fear of starvation.

Locke was luckier than Leroy Loughborough, as he apparently recovered from the episode. It isn't clear what happened to George Loughborough, but his lighthouse-keeping career was no doubt over. This story begs for more details, but few can be found. One can't help wondering whether George Loughborough truly abandoned his duties out of concern for a sick aunt, or if Keeper Locke was an innocent victim of brotherly revenge against the government. The missing parts of this story may well be stranger than what we actually know.

In his book *Northeast Lights: Lighthouses and Lightships, Rhode Island to Cape May, New Jersey*, Robert Bachand described another near-tragedy involving a Green's Ledge assistant keeper. In February 1917 Frank Thompson had gone ashore for supplies and was returning in the station's rowboat when he became trapped by ice floes. Thompson found himself drifting helplessly, but was saved thanks to the frantic phone calls of a South Norwalk resident. Lighthouse Service officials in turn contacted a local towing company, and the crew of a tug performed the rescue for $50.

The light was automated in 1972 and the last Coast Guard keepers were reassigned. A 1986 survey of the structure by John Milner Associates of West Chester, Pennsylvania, showed that it had gone through many changes. The stanchions and lower gallery roof had long ago been removed after deterioration due to lack of maintenance, and the main deck floor had been covered in a "cementious" material. New pipe stanchions and steel cable had replaced the old stanchions and railings. The interior woodwork had been stripped from the watchroom and lantern levels.

The caisson was described as having some structural problems, including a major crack on its east side. The crack may date back to the punishing hurricane of September 21, 1938. Two retaining bands had been secured around the caisson for added support.

Four Coast Guard lightkeepers bring supplies onto the rocks next to the lighthouse at Green's Ledge in 1950. Left to right: Arthur Backer, Willis Twiford, Edmond La Bonte, and Ralph Olsen. *U.S. Coast Guard photo.*

The report also mentioned that the lighthouse had become infested with rats and recommended that "some exterminating measures should be taken to remove the rodents and enable the Coast Guard personnel to maintain the light without apprehension."

Since that time the Coast Guard has performed basic maintenance, including sandblasting and repainting. The tower appears to be in fair condition at present, but a full restoration, including the replication of lost elements, would be extremely costly. A full engineering study would be needed to accurately assess the condition of the caisson.

It appears that the lighthouse will soon be made available to a suitable steward under the National Historic Lighthouse Preservation Act of 2000. We can only hope that someone will step forward and speak up for this slightly battered "sparkplug." Meanwhile, a solar-powered, rotating VRB-25 optic (a popular and reliable system manufactured in New Zealand) continues to display alternating red and white flashes every 12 seconds.

This lighthouse is difficult to see up close except by private boat, but you can see it distantly from Sheffield Island.

CHAPTER 4

Sheffield Island Lighthouse in August 2004. *Photo by the author.*

4

Sheffield Island Light

(Norwalk Island Light)
1827, 1868

Its prime location on Long Island Sound at the mouth of the Norwalk River led Norwalk to become a center for coastal and West Indies trade, but the many islands and reefs near the river's mouth formed an obstacle course for mariners.

The 16 Norwalk Islands have history and romance to match any similar archipelago in the Northeast. Such luminaries as playwright Lillian Hellman and producer Billy Rose spent time on the islands, and there are persistent legends of pirates and treasure. But much of the chain's colorful past and present revolves around 53-acre Sheffield Island and its lighthouse. In official documents the lighthouse was usually referred to as Norwalk Island or Norwalk Islands Light, but local citizens know it as Sheffield Island Light.

The island first appears in the public record in 1690, when an Indian chief named Winnipauk deeded it to Rev. Thomas Hanford. Hanford died three years later and his family took little interest in their offshore holdings. A little more than a century later the island was bought by Joseph F. White of Danbury, who sold it in 1804 to Capt. Robert Sheffield.

Sheffield was originally from Stonington, Connecticut, and at the age of 25 had been the captain of a vessel captured in the Revolution. He married a *Mayflower* descendent from Saybrook named Temperance Doty, and the two eventually moved to the island off Norwalk Harbor with their seven children in 1804.

In 1810 one of the Sheffields' daughters, also named Temperance, married a family friend, widower Gershom Burr Smith. Smith later bought the island from his father-in-law and became the owner of several of the other islands as well. Gershom and Temperance Smith had twelve children born between 1811 and 1836.

The enterprising Gershom Smith opened a tavern on the island. An 1818 ad in the *Norwalk Gazette* read:

> *The subscriber having opened a House of Entertainment, on Norwalk Island, at the mouth of the harbour, can accommodate Parties, wishing to take an excursion on the water, with the best of Liquors and Provisions. Large Parties are desired to send previous notice.*

Smith managed his islands as a farm, clearing trees and planting wheat, corn, and potatoes. He also had a number of cows, which reportedly were made to swim from Wilson's Point in Norwalk, guided by men in boats. According to tradition, the cows would walk over the sandbars that connected some of the islands at low tide. At milking time, Smith rowed from island to island to milk every last wayward cow.

Gershom and Temperance Smith. *Photo from the Norwalk Seaport Association Collection.*

In 1826 officials decided a lighthouse was needed to guide vessels past the hazards on the approach to the harbor. On May 18, 1826, Congress appropriated $4,000 for the lighthouse. Specifications called for a 34-foot conical stone tower with an octagonal iron lantern, along with a one-story, 20- by 34-foot stone dwelling with an attached 10- by 12-foot kitchen. The lighting apparatus was to consist of 10 lamps with ten 16-inch reflectors. The federal government bought three acres for the lighthouse at the eastern end of the island from Gershom Smith, who was appointed keeper in June 1827.

A report by Lt. George M. Bache in 1838 described the tower as being in good repair. Bache found Gershom Smith's work as keeper satisfactory. Bache wrote:

> *The lighting apparatus consists of 10 lamps, with parabolic reflectors, arranged in two clusters. . . . One of the clusters of lamps shows a red light, which is produced by placing a pane of colored glass in front of each of its lights and reflectors; two of these panes of glass are broken.*
>
> *The dwelling-house is of stone, and is in a good state of repair. The oil is stored in the cellar of the dwelling and in the tower.*

Bache also noted that the keeper had adjusted the revolving mechanism for the light. The entire apparatus was supposed to rotate so that the white light was interrupted by a red flash every two minutes and 45 seconds, but Smith had changed the interval to 66 seconds. He told

Bache that there had been complaints that there was too much time between flashes.

Things slipped considerably in a short period if one believes a letter to the editor in the *Norwalk Gazette* in December 1842. A writer identifying himself only as "Neptune" deemed the light a failure, saying:

> *In approaching the harbor the Island is usually seen for a considerable length of time before the light, and a proximity of six or seven miles, sometimes much nearer, is necessary to catch a glimpse of the latter. . . . Is not such a light more dangerous and disadvantageous than none at all?*

About two weeks later another writer calling himself "Coaster" questioned Neptune's observations. But he was also critical of the lighthouse:

> *The light spoken of is faulty in point of its fixtures which have been in use fifteen years, since the erection of the light and are much worn. Again, the Light House is not high enough into many feet to be seen at any considerable distance; yet compares well with other lights not having a greater elevation.*

Gershom Smith was removed as keeper in early 1845, apparently for political reasons, as was common in that era. John Tyler was president at the time and Smith was obviously not a supporter. The *Norwalk Gazette* reported that the keeper had been "Tylerized." Smith's replacement, Lewis Whitlock, "though a good-natured, good-for-nothing creature," according to the *Gazette*, "is about the last object, in which God's image has not been wholly obliterated, that we should have selected for an officer of the United States of America."

Whitlock arrived as keeper in January 1845. Apparently no improvements had been made to the lighting apparatus and the clockwork mechanism that rotated the lamps, and Whitlock complained to the authorities. A *Norwalk Gazette* story on July 30, 1845, seems to substantiate Whitlock's complaints:

> A Faithful Servant—*It is related of the keeper of the Light House on Norwalk Island, that the machinery by which the lights revolve, was recently broken, and he was obliged to send to this city to effect repairs. In the mean time, fearing that some mariner might be deceived, by the lights becoming stationary, he mounted regularly into the top, for several nights and from dark until sunrise, kept the lights revolving, by turning them with his hand! A most commendable discharge of duty.*

An 1850 inspection revealed that there had finally been a decision to install new reflectors. The report also included unusually personal comments about Keeper Whitlock:

> *Light-house has been recently whitewashed, and the lantern painted; wood work is sound. . . . Lantern apparatus was clean, and so was everything in and about the light-house; lamps are in good burning order, but the reflectors are poor. I ordered a set for this light-house of 13 inches, but those that were sent me were 14 inches; consequently, had none to put on. Clock runs well. Keeper is alone, entirely so, and everything he has in the house is out of fix; nothing is done right; nothing is as it should be. Poor man, and miserable, and will continue so without a wife.*

By 1855 a new system with six lamps and 21-inch parabolic reflectors had been installed, replaced by a new fourth-order Fresnel lens in 1857. The new lens improved the light's visibility, but the tower was always regarded as too short. With increased shipping in the area after the Civil War, a decision was made to build a new combined lighthouse and dwelling. An appropriation of $12,000 was made for that purpose on March 2, 1867.

Sheffield Island Lighthouse in the late nineteenth century. *From the collection of Edward Rowe Snow, courtesy of Dorothy Bicknell.*

The style of the lighthouse finished the following year is the same as that of five others built in southern New England and Long Island Sound in the same period. It consists of a two-and-one-half-story, 10-room dwelling built of granite blocks, 30 by 32 feet with a 16- by 18-foot kitchen wing at the rear. At the front end of the peak of the roof is a cast-iron light tower rising to a height of 46 feet. The fourth-order lens from the old tower was apparently transferred to the new one. The old tower was demolished and its site is now underwater. The original stone keeper's dwelling still stands to the rear of the 1868 lighthouse.

The rest of the nineteenth century passed fairly uneventfully at the lighthouse. Samuel Armour arrived as keeper in 1886. In 1901 Armour contracted typhoid, apparently from drinking water from the station's cistern that had been contaminated by the privy. Armour's wife helped to keep the station running properly during her husband's illness, and a temporary assistant keeper was hired. Armour recovered to become the first keeper of the New Haven Outer Breakwater Light (Sperry Light) in 1902.

The local oystering industry reached its peak in the late nineteenth and early twentieth centuries, and this period saw a number of improvements in the vicinity of Norwalk Harbor. The channel was dredged and it was decided that a light on Green's Ledge would be a better warning of the dangerous obstruction there than the old light on Sheffield Island. The 1868 lighthouse was retired as an aid to navigation.

After the light was discontinued on February 15, 1902, the lighthouse remained a shore station for the keepers at Green's Ledge for a few years. In 1914 the government sold it along with the 1827 keeper's cottage to Thorsten O. Stabell, longtime custodian of the Norwalk Yacht Club. The property remained in the Stabell family for many years, but it was made available to local organizations for outings.

In July 1986 the Stabells offered the lighthouse property for sale, and in late December the property was sold for $700,000 to the Norwalk Seaport Association (NSA). A total of $160,000 was paid immediately, including $100,000 from the city's Island Acquisition Fund. The NSA was originally given three years to come up with the additional $540,000. It was a daring move, as the building was also in need of much expensive restoration.

In the summer of 1987 the NSA opened the lighthouse to visitors on a limited basis. The following year they hired graduate student Andy Siegel as summer caretaker. Like keepers of old, Siegel once went to the rescue of some boys whose skiff had broken down near the island, giving them a tow to the mainland.

In the late 1980s the lighthouse was refurbished largely by volunteers and local contractors, including Cutrone/Toni. About 18,000 pounds of new roofing slates were ferried to the island, and Norwalk Marine Contractors donated equipment and labor for the construction of a new pier. The ongoing restoration efforts received a huge boost in November 1989, when $300,000 earmarked for restoration was secured from the State Department of Economic Development. Interior renovations, including plastering, painting, and refinishing, started in 1993.

Pat O'Shaughnessy was hired as caretaker for the summer of 1989. The tall, ruddy O'Shaughnessy looked more like a lighthouse keeper than a high school English teacher, which he was the rest of the year. That year the Seaport Association started running a regular ferry to the island, and O'Shaughnessy doubled as a tour guide. He returned to the island as "keeper" each summer for eight years.

Like so many islands and lighthouses, this one has its rumors of a ghostly presence. In 1991 archaeologist Karen Orawsky was working on Sheffield Island. One day as she approached the island in a boat, she heard "hypnotic and mystical" music coming from the island, with no apparent source. She also heard a nonexistent foghorn and distant cries for help. Some believe the music could be attributed to the spirit of Capt. Sheffield, who played the long spell, an unusual instrument somewhat like an oversized violin played with porcupine quills.

Late in 1992 a storm slammed into the island, sending waves crashing into the lighthouse foundation. Windows were broken and the basement was flooded with more than four feet of water. Ten feet of shoreline on the south side near the lighthouse was chewed away by the storm. In 1996 Hurricane Fran caused further significant erosion. During the following year work was done to slow the erosion, with the installation of gabions (wire mesh frameworks filled with stones) and the planting of beach grass and roses.

By late 1996 the NSA faced possible foreclosure on the property. In the summer of 1998 it announced a $1 million capital campaign, with the aim of retiring the $391,000 mortgage, establishing a trust fund, and improving the lighthouse facilities and programs. Mayor Frank Esposito and four former mayors of Norwalk gathered on the steps of the Norwalk Concert Hall to draw attention to the cause.

As the deadline loomed, NSA officials presented a check for $191,458 to National Loan Investors of Oklahoma City. The First National Union Bank of Norwalk followed with a $200,000 bridge loan to stall the foreclosure. But this loan still needed to be paid back. In July 2000 it was announced that the debt had been reduced to $30,000. Finally on September 11, 2000, the long-anticipated goal was reached. About 150 supporters of the NSA ventured to the lighthouse for a mortgage burning ceremony.

Seasonal caretakers are still hired yearly by the NSA. The caretakers also manage a crew of volunteers and paid staffers who help maintain the property and give tours. The 2003 "keeper" was South African native David Graaf, who lived in the original keeper's cottage. Graaf's wife, Gillian, is a New York City business analyst, and their two children spent much of the summer on the island.

The 2004 caretaker was lifelong Norwalk resident and Coast Guard Auxiliarist Don Burr, who found evidence of a possible relationship to the first keeper, Gershom Burr Smith. Burr first fell in love with lighthouses as a boy while staying at his grandparents' home in Rockland, Maine, where the light from Rockland Breakwater Lighthouse entered nightly through his bedroom window. Burr's first season on the island was such a success that the NSA has signed him on as caretaker indefinitely.

Aside from the lighthouse, the rest of Sheffield Island has its own colorful past. In 1912 New York architect Alfred Mestre purchased a bungalow on the island's east side, and proceeded to add a large stucco house and make the property into a Spanish villa complete with pool and sunken garden.

Robert L. Corby of the Fleischmann's Yeast fortune bought the estate in the 1930s and created a resort with a golf course and tennis courts. The "Island Club" even had a day care center for children and a stable with polo ponies and racehorses. This venture failed quickly because of the dearth of freshwater on the island, and the former golf course was used for a time as a landing strip.

The property was later owned by James H. Rand of the Rand Corporation. The main villa was mostly destroyed in a suspicious fire, thought by some to have been started by Rand's wife after she caught him in a compromising situation. Some of the ruins of this once-magnificent property can still be seen near the shore.

Today 47 acres of Sheffield Island are part of the Stewart B. McKinney National Wildlife Refuge, with a public walking trail and observation platform. Visitors are likely to spot several types of herons and egrets, as well as deer and raccoons.

It's been a long, hard struggle for the NSA and supporters of this lighthouse, and it's far from finished. More funds are needed to complete the restoration of the lighthouse and to develop educational programs. The biggest fundraiser for the NSA is its annual Oyster Festival, launched in 1978, which has featured big-name entertainment such as the Charlie Daniels Band and Little Richard. Besides the lighthouse, the proceeds from the festival help the association provide environmental education programs for more than 10,000 local preschool and elementary school children each year.

You can visit Sheffield Island and its lighthouse by taking the ferry from the Seaport Dock next to the Maritime Aquarium in South Norwalk. For more information and schedules, visit the NSA Web site at www.seaport.org or call (203) 838-9444.

Peck's Ledge Light in 2000. ***Photo by the author.***

Peck's Ledge Light

(Peck Ledge Light)
1906

In 1614 Dutch explorer Adrian Block observed the Norwalk Islands in western Long Island Sound and noted them in his log. This scenic cluster of 16 islands and many smaller rocks has long been a stumbling block for boat traffic heading in and out of Norwalk Harbor.

The first lighthouse in the vicinity was placed on Sheffield Island, the largest island, in 1827. That light was replaced by Green's Ledge Light to the southwest in 1902. Peck's Ledge Light was added four years later at the northeast end of the archipelago to warn of dangerous Peck's Ledge to the southwest as well as a shoal extending north from Goose Island.

Requests for a lighthouse at the east end of the islands began in 1896, and a $10,000 appropriation was made in 1901. It was decided that the lighthouse should be large enough to contain living quarters for two keepers, necessitating an additional $29,000.

An article in the *Norwalk Hour* in May 1905, after work on the lighthouse had already commenced, reported that many local mariners were displeased. "It is proposed to locate the new light at the end of Peck's Ledge, northeast of Goose Island, thus making it a harbor light entirely," stated the article. It continued:

> *Vessels coming from the east or west will only be fooled by it, they say, and will be doubly liable to land on the long and dangerous ledge running northeast for a mile from Cockenoe Island and ending with George's Rock, or when coming from the west to run on the rocks outside of Copp's or Goose Islands. The new light will be of no practical use, according to those who follow the water, until Cockenoe Island reef is passed and the boat practically starts to enter the harbor. A dolphin [a light or marker on pilings] or buoy could do the job at 1/8 the cost.*

But it was too late to change sites. During the summer of 1905 a cast-iron foundation cylinder was assembled, sunk into place, and filled with concrete. Construction of the cast-iron superstructure proceeded the following spring, and the light went into operation on July 10, 1906, with a fourth-order Fresnel lens 61 feet above the water showing a two-second white flash every 10 seconds. A fog signal operating on compressed air was also installed. The first principal keeper was George Bardwell, at a salary of $600 per year.

The brick-lined interior of the 54-foot lighthouse included a basement, three floors of living and storage space, and a wood-lined watchroom topped by a cast-iron lantern. The first floor served as a combination living room/dining room/kitchen, the second floor as the keepers' sleeping quarters, and the third floor was used for storage. The company that built Peck's Ledge Lighthouse—Toomey Brothers of Guilford, Connecticut—had four years earlier built Hooper Island Lighthouse, a similar structure in the Chesapeake Bay.

According to Robert Bachand's *Northeast Lights: Lighthouses and Lightships, Rhode Island to Cape May, New Jersey*, the lighthouse narrowly escaped destruction by fire in February 1913. It seems Keeper Conrad Hawk (or Haake) was working on his lobster traps and absentmindedly left a tub of tar on a newspaper near the kitchen stove. He left to tend a nearby light at Grassy Hammock, and returned to see thick smoke pouring from the lighthouse. Hawk used a clam rake to get the flaming tub of tar into the ocean and managed to quickly douse the remaining flames with seawater.

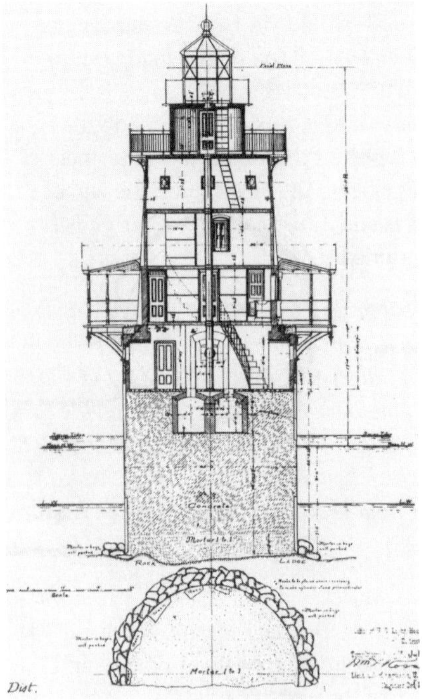

Plans for Peck Ledge Light. *Courtesy of U.S. Coast Guard.*

During a storm late in the afternoon of December 5, 1921, the canal steamer *J. C. Austin* of Brooklyn, New York, developed a leak near Green's Ledge Light. The vessel's pumps failed to work, and a pipe in the boiler also sprang a leak. The four crewmen escaped to a lifeboat and drifted until the keepers at Peck's Ledge spotted them.

Keeper Charles Kenney and two assistants, George H. Barker and George Clark, set out in heavy seas in the small lighthouse boat and

Peck's Ledge Light in its early years. *U.S. Coast Guard photo.*

rescued the crew of the *Austin*. When they arrived back at the lighthouse, the crewmen were so exhausted that the keepers had to carry them up the ladder. The following day an oyster boat took the crewmen ashore. "Keeper Kenney was greatly thanked by the rescued men for his timely assistance," reported the *Norwalk Hour*, "for they might have otherwise perished in the storm."

The light at Peck's Ledge was automated in 1933, bringing to a close its brief 27-year history as a staffed station. Despite minimal maintenance, a 1989 survey found the structure in "fair" condition. The caisson had developed some cracks and corrosion, and the interior displayed corrosion, cracked masonry, and evidence of feathered intruders. The next year the crew of the Coast Guard cutter *Redwood* sandblasted and repainted the caisson. They scraped paint from the interior brick, cleaned the interior, and covered the windows.

A 15-foot vertical ladder provides access to the light, making it difficult to service. According to Michael Allen, chief engineer for U.S. Coast Guard Aids to Navigation Team Long Island Sound, the Coast Guard gear is bulky and heavy. "On a flat sea day we can tie the boat up to the ladder, but if there are any swells we can only drop technicians off on the ladder one at a time. It's hairy sometimes."

In February 2004 the Coast Guard announced plans to install 100 tons of granite riprap around the east side of the tower, along with an eight-foot-wide section of step-cut stones on the west side to facilitate access from the bow of the Coast Guard's maintenance boat.

Ownership of this lighthouse is expected to be transferred soon from the Coast Guard to a qualified new owner under the National Historic Lighthouse Preservation Act of 2000.

Peck's Ledge Lighthouse can be seen distantly from Calf Pasture Beach in Norwalk, but you need to be in a boat for a good, close look. At present there are no regular public cruises that pass close by. The 250-mm modern optic in the lantern is solar powered and displays a flashing green light every two and a half seconds.

Penfield Reef Light in 2002. *Photo by the author.*

6

Penfield Reef Light

1874

The shoal that extends more than a mile from Penfield Beach in Fairfield was long a scourge to mariners traveling by on Long Island Sound or heading to the harbors at Black Rock and Bridgeport. Even with the lighthouse's modern VRB-25 optic flashing its warning today, hardly a season passes without several boats running aground here. Tradition holds that this was once solid land that supported the pasturing of cattle, hence the names "Cows" and "Calves" for two prominent rocky parts of the shoal.

In 1864 the steamer *Rip Van Winkle* ran into the rocks with many passengers, and a major tragedy was narrowly averted. In the winter of 1866–67 alone, four more vessels ran into the shoal. The dangerous location was marked only by a day beacon and two buoys, and local merchants and mariners clamored for a lighthouse. Captain D. C. Constable of the Board of Light-House Commissioners called the Cows "the most dangerous locality, during fogs and snow-storms, upon Long Island sound."

On April 22, 1868, Joseph Lederle, acting lighthouse engineer of the Third District, wrote to Adm. W. B. Shubrick of the Lighthouse Board, agreeing that a lighthouse was needed "to guide clear of the shoal extending from Fairfield." He recommended that the lighthouse be built "on the plan approved by the board for the Hudson river," adding that a powerful fog signal was also essential.

The Lighthouse Board asked for $55,000 for a light station on Penfield Reef, to be built in water about five feet deep. When Lederle referred to the Hudson River stations, he had in mind the newly designed Esopus Meadows Lighthouse that would be built in 1871. Esopus Meadows, like most similar lighthouses, consisted of a dwelling of wood-frame construction with an integral cast-iron tower. But the dwelling at Penfield Reef would be built of stone. In terms of design and construction, a close sibling of this lighthouse was the Sabin Point Lighthouse built on the Providence River, in Rhode Island, in 1871.

There was no immediate action, but finally on July 15, 1870, Congress appropriated $30,000, followed by an additional $25,000 on March 3, 1871. The 1872 Annual Report of the Lighthouse Board described the early stages of construction and hinted at some difficulties involving the contractor for the granite pier upon which the lighthouse would stand:

> *The foundation of riprap was laid during the previous season, and stood uninjured throughout the winter gales. . . . The contractor of the pier, owing to his want of adequate means, has delayed the work, and the forbearance of the engineer toward him has alone prevented the annulling of his contract and the commencement of suit to recover the amount of the bonds.*

The granite riprap foundation for the lighthouse was 108 feet in diameter. On top of this, the 18-foot-tall pier was constructed of cut granite in nine courses, 48½ feet in diameter at the base and 46½ feet at the top. The conical ring of granite was filled with concrete, with a cavity left near the top to serve as the lighthouse's basement. The pier was based on the one designed for Race Rock Light in Fisher's Island Sound, New York. The 28-foot-square dwelling with a mansard roof was built centrally on the pier. Between 1898 and 1902 builders added more than 1,200 tons of granite riprap as extra protection around the foundation.

Race Rock, Penfield Reef, and Stratford Shoal (1877) would prove to be among the last offshore masonry lighthouses on masonry foundations built in the United States before cast-iron towers on cylindrical cast-iron caissons came into vogue.

In 1874 the Lighthouse Board reported that both the tower and the dwelling had been completed, and that the beacon had been lighted for the first time on January 16. A mechanized fog bell had been installed as well.

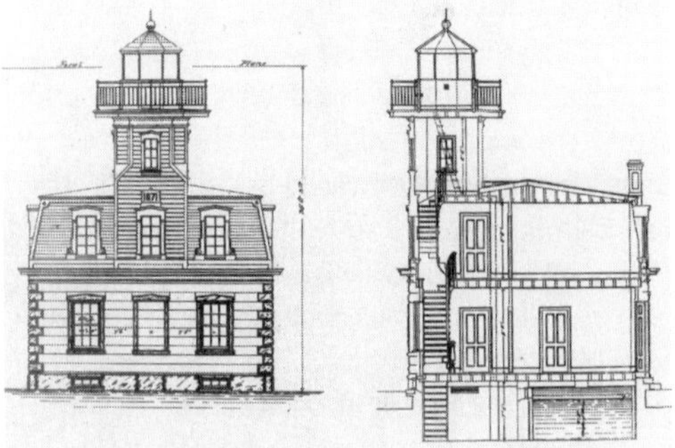

Plans for Penfield Reef Light. *Courtesy of U.S. Coast Guard.*

The granite walls of the first floor are lined with brick. The second floor originally contained four bedrooms, while the first consisted of a kitchen, living room, and oil room. The second story and light tower are of wood-frame construction and the

Nineteenth-century engraving of Penfield Reef Light. *From the author's collection.*

tower at the watchroom level is octagonal. Above that is an octagonal cast-iron lantern, which originally held a fourth-order Fresnel lens. The lens revolved by means of a clockwork mechanism that keepers had to wind by hand. The light flashed red, 51 feet above sea level.

The first keeper, George Tomlinson, remained only two years. Turnover at the offshore station was high, with many keepers and assistants remaining only a year or two. William Jones was head keeper starting in 1880 at a salary of $500 yearly, and his wife, Pauline, was his assistant at $400 per year. Neil Martin, formerly at Race Rock and Stamford Harbor, was keeper from 1882 to 1891. His wife, Jane, served as an assistant keeper during some of that time. Jane died in March 1886, and Keeper Martin received a cold letter from the Lighthouse Depot in Tompkinsville, New York: "Find a competent man to take your place, and then leave of absence to attend the burial of your wife is hereby granted you."

It was often harrowing getting to and from the lighthouse, especially in winter. Nelson B. Allen, an assistant keeper, had a hair-raising experience in late January of 1888, as the January 30 *New York Times* reported:

> *He came ashore in the afternoon after medicine for his wife, and started on his return at 5 o'clock. His boat got wedged between two*

large cakes of ice which were drifting southward. He was unable to release it. After floating about for five hours he was rescued by the steamer City of New Haven *and transferred to a tug which had been sent out in search of him. He was exhausted, and his limbs were frost-bitten.*

The saddest incident in the lighthouse's history took place nearly three decades later. On December 22, 1916, Keeper Fred A. Jordan (sometimes spelled Jordon) left the lighthouse at 20 minutes past noon to row ashore. There were high seas and strong winds, but the keeper badly wanted to join his family for Christmas and to give his handmade presents to his children. Assistant Keeper Rudolph Iten watched from the lighthouse as Jordan pushed his boat through the waves.

About a hundred yards from the lighthouse, Jordan's boat capsized. He clung to the boat and signaled for Iten to lower the station's remaining boat and come to his aid. Iten tried valiantly to do so, but the steadily increasing waves and wind made it impossible. He finally got under way about 1:00 p.m., but by that time Jordan had drifted a mile and a half to the southwest. Iten said later:

I did my level best to reach him, but I hadn't pulled more than half a mile when the wind changed to the southwest, making a headwind and an outgoing tide, against which I couldn't move the heavy boat. I had to give up, and returned to the station in a regular gale. From the station I sent distress signals to passing ships, but none answered. At three o'clock I lost sight of the drifting boat. The poor fellow's body wasn't found until three months later. He was a fine fellow, was Fred.

Iten was absolved of any blame for Jordan's death. He was promoted to head keeper and would remain for more than a decade. A May 14, 1922, article by F. A. Barrow in the *Bridgeport Sunday Post* offered an intimate glimpse of life at Penfield Reef. Iten lived with two assistants, Walter Harper and Arthur Bender. Each of the men, all World War I veterans, got eight days off each month. When Barrow entered, a "lively little dog came bounding and barking a welcome. This was Penfield, or Pen for short."

The conversation after Barrow's arrival revolved around the "merits of various washing and scouring powders," prompting the writer to remark, "I would suggest to any suffragette looking for a husband who could keep house while she was attending business or lectures, that she might do well to choose a lighthouse keeper." Barrow asked the keeper how the work was divided between the men. He replied, "We stand watches. This is my watch. At one in the morning Arthur goes on duty. The regular work we share, washing, scrubbing and cooking; and we can all cook, too—you wait and see."

Barrow learned later that "the boast in regard to cooking was not an idle one" when he was treated to "steak and noodles a la Penfield." Dessert was "a beautiful pink cake" that Arthur Bender had won in Fairfield.

The living room had green walls decorated with photos of all the Allied generals of World War I. There were a table, several chairs, a desk, and a "graphonola" with records. Reading material included poems by Robert Burns and Henry Wadsworth Longfellow, and a copy of Edgar Allan Poe's "The Gold Bug." The bedrooms on the second floor were "comfortably but not luxuriously furnished," the article reported, with "cot-beds" all neatly made.

For heat, the lighthouse had three stoves, with eight tons of coal and three cords of wood for winter fuel. Barrow wondered how the men dealt with the ice on the station in winter. Bender explained that they sprinkled ashes wherever they walked outside to avoid sliding into the sound.

The lighthouse's sturdy construction served it well in the brutal storms that occasionally swept through Long Island Sound. Keeper Iten described the violent gale of October 24, 1917, to Barrow:

> *The waves dashed against the place and shook it to the foundations. They broke above the pier, smashed glass and sashes, and the spray went clean over the light. Wild? I'll say it was. I had a new motor-boat that my father-in-law and I had purchased together. We had taken the engine out for an overhauling. Well, the waves caught that nice, new boat and made kindling wood of it. . . . I was mighty glad at that time that the light was on a good foundation.*

A few years later another writer visited Keeper Iten and a conversation in the wee hours of the morning turned decidedly macabre. "They say that all lighthouse keepers are mad," said Iten as a preface to the following chilling tale, told against the background of the whispering wind and the gentle wash of the waves.

> *You ask if there has ever been anything in the nature of a supernatural occurrence at this lighthouse. Well, all light keepers are more or less hard-boiled and not given over to stretches of imagination. While I don't deny or admit the theory of ghosts, something happened here one night that seemed to point to the establishment of the fact that there are such things as supernatural visitations.*

Iten recounted the accidental death of Keeper Jordan in December 1916, then continued:

> *Some days later on what was one of the worst nights in the history of Penfield, and the waves were dashing over the lantern, I was awakened—I was off duty—by a strange feeling that someone was in my room. Sitting up I distinctly saw a gray, phosphorescent figure emerging from the room formerly occupied by Fred Jordan. It hovered at the top of the stairs, and then disappeared in the darkness below. Thinking it was the assistant keeper I called to know if anything was the matter, but he answered me from the lens room that all was well.*
>
> *Much puzzled, I went downstairs and to my consternation I saw lying on the table the log-book of the lighthouse, with the page recording the drowning of Poor Jordan staring me in the face!*
>
> *I have seen the semblance of the figure several times since and so have the others, and we are all prepared to take an affidavit to that effect. Something comes here, that we are positive. There is an old saying, "What the Reef takes, the Reef will give back." Poor Jordan's body was recovered not long after his drowning, and in the pocket of his coat was found a note addressed to me—which he probably forgot to leave before he started on his fateful ride in that rough sea—instructing me to complete the entries of that morning—the day he died—as they were not brought up to date.*

An undated article in the Bridgeport Public Library claims that, on stormy nights, "the specter of the reef is said to be flitting among the rocks, poised on the rail of the gallery that surrounds the lantern or swaying, as if in agony, among the black and jagged rocks that surround the base of the light." The article tells the story of a power yacht that ran into trouble but was "piloted through the breakers to safety by a strange man who suddenly appeared amid the surf . . . in a row-boat." And then there were the two boys who were fishing near the reef when their canoe capsized, throwing them into the sea. A man appeared "from out of the rocks" and pulled them to safety. When they came to, they entered the lighthouse expecting to thank their savior, but he was nowhere to be found.

Keeper Iten said that he and the other keepers had performed 27 rescues in his years at Penfield Reef, including canoeists trying to cross the shoal and exhausted swimmers. Once the keepers towed a motorboat full of people stuck on the reef and repaired the boat's rudder. For their trouble, the men were given the paltry reward of one dollar. "Of course, we never accept monetary remuneration," said Iten, "but the value put by the leader of the party on our lives and his company—at one dollar—well, it was amusing."

Shipping mishaps and rescues around the lighthouse were commonplace through its years as a staffed station. In September 1916 nine barges of the Blue Line Company piled up on part of the reef, a location henceforth known as the Blue Line Graveyard. Another time a coal freighter ran right into the lighthouse, dislodging some of the riprap stones and making the keepers think an earthquake was in progress. And Iten told the story of a small boat that hit the reef in broad daylight The skipper lodged an official complaint about the light being "too dim."

The Lighthouse Service Bulletin of February 1, 1929, reported, "William A. Shackley, first assistant keeper of Penfield Reef Light Station, Conn., on January 19 rendered assistance to a scow which was in distress in the vicinity of the station during a heavy sea. The keeper left the light station at 3 o'clock in the morning, took the captain and his wife off the scow, and brought them to the light station and provided for them overnight." The following year on November 1, the bulletin described another rescue: "E. T. Pastorini, second assistant keeper, Penfield Reef Light Station, Conn., rescued three men who were clinging to the bottom of an overturned rowboat, during a severe storm on October 10."

Seen here in a 1933 photo, George Petzolt was alone at the lighthouse through the great hurricane of September 21, 1938. *Courtesy of Harold Petzolt and* Lighthouse Digest.

William Hardwick came to Penfield Reef in 1932 after time as a keeper at Stratford Shoal, Peck's Ledge, Bridgeport Harbor, and Faulkner's Island lights. A native of Yorkshire, England, Hardwick had come to the United States with his family in 1885. Eight years later he went to sea as a teenager on a fishing boat in the North Sea. Hardwick's travels as a fisherman and in the merchant marines took him far and wide. According to a 1941 article in the *Bridgeport Sunday Post*, he claimed that once, off Sicily, he heard the song of the sirens—a traditional bad omen. Two days later his vessel was struck by a giant wave and 22 crewmen died.

In late December 1935 at Penfield Reef Light, Hardwick said that he heard the call of the sirens for a second time, a low, eerie music that froze him in the tower. The next day the area was ravaged by a blizzard, with a Japanese steamer going aground on Penfield Reef and scores of other wrecks in the vicinity.

On September 21, 1938, the day the worst New England hurricane of the twentieth century struck, Hardwick was rowing a 12-foot skiff out to the lighthouse as the winds picked up and the seas swelled. He hastily retreated to Fairfield, where he spent the night. Another lone keeper, George Petzolt, survived the night at the lighthouse. According to his son, Harold, George feared he might not live as he watched boats, telephone poles, and other debris sweep past.

One day in 1941 Hardwick left in a rowboat for his shore leave, fighting his way through choppy seas and a brisk wind. Arriving at his cottage on Reef Road in Fairfield and removing his oilskins, he said to his wife, "Millie, I'm through with this job." A week later he retired after 23 years in the Lighthouse Service. It was reported that his pastimes included "fooling around in the garden and scaring his grandchildren with his tales of the sea."

George Petzolt's son Harold remembers sitting in his mother's lap as his father rowed the family out to the lighthouse in the 1930s. George would sing an old sea shanty as he rowed: "See saw Marjorie Daw, Johnny shall have a new master, He shall get a penny a day, 'cause he can row no faster." Later Harold was allowed to row, but his father would deliberately rock the boat as he sang. This was designed to teach the boy how to row in rough conditions, and the training came in handy when father and son were caught in a squall on the way to the lighthouse. As waves crashed over the little boat, the two rowed together to safety as they sang, "See saw Marjorie Daw. . . . "

Harold also remembers family ghost story sessions at the lighthouse. One night, just as his sister was saying that the lighthouse's resident ghost liked to make noises like a ship's horn to get the keepers to go outside on the gallery, a loud horn outside made everyone jump. Soon horns could be heard from a number of boats outside. Keepers Petzolt and Hardwick looked at each other, puzzled. They were sure the light was on and they couldn't imagine the reason for all the horn blowing. George Petzolt asked his son to take a look up into the tower to see if the light was burning, and it was.

George ran out to the rocks, though, and noticed that the light couldn't be seen from there. He came back inside and quickly went up into the lantern room. "Get blankets and towels, hurry!" he yelled to those below. As it turned out, the outside of the lantern glass was completely covered with a swarm of insects, which Harold Petzolt says were praying mantises. The insects were soon driven away by the frantic swiping of towels and blankets against the glass.

In its later years as a staffed station under the Coast Guard, three men were assigned to Penfield Reef, with two on duty at one time. The men had two weeks on followed by one week off. One of the last keepers was C. J. Stites, who later became Bridgeport's senior deputy harbormaster. In an article in the *Fairfield Citizen-News*, he said that visitors were generally not allowed, but sometimes people did stop by with food or bits of news.

The crew put a sign saying "Send newspapers" in a window. "Newspapers were worth their weight in gold," Stites said. A lobsterman sometimes passed by and threw the day's paper near the lighthouse door, and one time a helicopter flew by and someone dumped a load of old newspapers on the roof.

Stites said holidays at the lighthouse were tough, especially the Fourth of July, when the men could hear music from Bridgeport's Seaside Park. Clark Ellison was also among the last Coast Guard keepers, and his memories dispel many notions of the romance of lighthouse life:

> *Most people believed it an adventure or possibly even romantic to be a "wickie." It was not. Most of the time it was nothing more than boring. . . . The light had an electric lamp and motor to turn the light, but the motor never worked. The light was kept in motion by a stack of weights on cables that had to be wound up on a drum, and the weights would lower through the floor and through a gear box that would spin the light, which floated in a brass vat of mercury. Or so I was told, as one could not see the mercury. If the weights touched the floor they would spin and twist the cable causing the motion to stop. . . .*
>
> *The radio almost never worked as it was an old tube type and tubes were hard to come by. We had to change at least one a week and [the Coast Guard station at] Eaton's Neck did not want to spend any unnecessary funds on the light, so we only received two or three a month. . . .*
>
> *Water came from a 180-foot buoy tender through a hose that was hauled by hand across the water—lots of fun when the tide was flowing. Do not ask where the septic field was as it did not exist. . . . On the first floor there was a kitchen and generator room. Penfield was the only light in our group that had shore power, so we only had one generator. How I hated the fog. The horn rattled the whole building, and my quarters were right above the horn.*

In the summer we fished and it was generally good, but in the winter the wind blew through the building. The curtains in the crew's quarters were seldom still. The dark green tiles on the galley deck were polished and waxed again and again as there was nothing else to do. The few times I managed to steal a TV from Eaton's Neck we did have TV to watch but as soon as I left, the guys from Eaton's Neck would retrieve the TV.

The water quality was such that it was boiled before drinking it. After a while we had five-gallon coolers with water, and we drained the cistern, scraped and repainted it.

One thing out of the ordinary at Penfield Reef, however, was the ghost. As a rule, Ellison didn't believe in ghosts, but then early one morning he and one other crewman were in the lighthouse:

I heard Stanley Blake walking up the stairs and decided to get up and have coffee with him, thinking it was just before sunrise. I got out of bed . . . and as I came out of the door I noticed there was no one coming up the stairs after all. It was at that time that Stan opened the door to his room and it was obvious he just woke up also.

He and I slinked around the light looking for the intruder and found no one. We were both sure someone had walked up the stairs as you could hear each step creak, one at a time. . . Now understand—we had visitors that would let themselves in at all hours of the day and night, but they always announced their arrival when they entered the kitchen. We had more visitations after that but did not get up to seek the ghost in person.

In late 1969 the Coast Guard announced plans to remove Penfield Reef Lighthouse and replace it with an automated light on a "pipe tower." The Coast Guard checked with Connecticut's State Historic Preservation Office, which knew of no historical significance attached to the structure. The president of the Fairfield Historical Society also had no objection to the Coast Guard's plans.

U.S. Representative Lowell Weicker and State Representative Stewart B. McKinney disagreed and asked the Coast Guard to reconsider. In late March of 1970 an announcement was made that the Coast Guard's new recommendation was to install a modern navigational aid at the site while keeping the lighthouse intact.

The new equipment was installed in 1971, and a decommissioning ceremony was held on September 4 of that year. At 1:00 p.m. there were "sail by" and "fly by" salutes to the lighthouse sponsored by the Penfield Power Squadron, and speakers included Weicker (by then a

U.S. senator) and McKinney (by then a congressman). Despite the September ceremony, the automation wasn't completed until early December 1971. The last crew on the station was reassigned and left on December 2.

The lighthouse slipped into disrepair following its automation. An inspection in 2000 noted that one of the main support beams had deteriorated, causing the lantern to tilt three degrees. In 2001 a contractor repaired water leaks in the lantern and repointed some of the building's mortar joints. The Coast Guard added a new lantern roof of stainless steel and did other renovations in 2003. There was word in late 2004 that a new support beam for the lantern was being installed.

In 2005 word is that Penfield Reef Lighthouse will soon be declared excess federal property and will be transferred to a suitable new steward under the provisions of the National Historic Lighthouse Preservation Act of 2000. The town of Fairfield has formed a lighthouse committee, and representatives have toured the lighthouse, finding the exterior in better shape than the interior. There are asbestos tiles on the floors and lead paint on the walls, and mold is prevalent.

Town officials are reportedly interested in obtaining ownership of the lighthouse, but they are hoping that funding for restoration will come from the community. The Fairfield Historical Society has taken a strong interest, but already has its hands full with the maintenance of six other historic structures. From all appearances, the local spirit is willing and advocates hope funding will be located.

Interestingly, the exact location of the lighthouse has been disputed: the Coast Guard says it's in Fairfield, as the shoal begins in Fairfield and the lighthouse is at the tip of the shoal, but a chart of local oyster grounds prepared by the state's Department of Agriculture puts the lighthouse in Bridgeport. Aside from such legal technicalities, let's hope that residents of both communities will work together for the preservation of the lighthouse, which was added to the National Register of Historic Places in 1990.

Penfield Reef's VRB-25 optic exhibits a red flash every six seconds, and the automated foghorn also continues to function as an official aid maintained by the Coast Guard.

It is possible to walk from Penfield Beach to the lighthouse at low tide—but it's not recommended. Local legend has it that a family of seven tried doing so and was caught on the bar by the incoming tide, never to be seen again. The lighthouse can be viewed from sightseeing cruises leaving Captain's Cove Seaport in Bridgeport. Call the Seaport office at (203) 335-1433 for more information.

CHAPTER 7

Black Harbor Light in August 2004. *Photo by the author.*

Black Rock Harbor Light

(Fayerweather Island Light)
1808, 1823

Black Rock village and harbor were part of the city of Fairfield for more than two centuries. The deep harbor thrived during the age of sail, but the steamships that came later were unable to navigate into the small harbor, and Bridgeport's shallower but more accessible harbor gained preeminence. Black Rock is today a section of Bridgeport.

The island now known as Fayerweather (or Fayerweather's) was sold by a Rev. Chauncey to farmer Benjamin Fayerweather in 1713. Several generations later, in July 1807, Daniel Fayerweather sold the 9.5-acre island for $200 to the federal government for the building of a lighthouse. Congress had appropriated $5,000 for the lighthouse in February 1807. Black Rock Harbor was sheltered by Fayerweather Island, once a much larger piece of land than it is now, making the island an ideal place for a light to guide vessels to safe harbor.

The first tower—wooden, octagonal, and 40 feet high to the base of the iron lantern—was in operation at the island's southern end by October 1808. The contractor was Abisha Woodward of New London, whose fame is secure in lighthouse annals for his building of the extant New London Harbor (1801) and Faulkner's Island (1802) lighthouses, among others. A small one-and-one-half-story keeper's dwelling was also erected, several hundred feet away from the tower on the other side of a marsh. A small stone oil house was also built.

The first keeper, John Maltbie of Fairfield, died after only five months on the island. The next keeper, Isaac Judson, a veteran of the American Revolution, died at the station in October 1814. After a stint by Daniel Wilson (or Willson), Stephen Tomlinson Moore became keeper in 1817. A former West Indies trader from Connecticut, Moore had been injured in a fall and could no longer travel at sea.

A tremendous storm laid the tower flat on September 3, 1821. The present 40-foot octagonal stone lighthouse was built for $2,300 and was in operation in 1823. A newspaper description, possibly written by one of the contractors, announced that the new tower was "prepared to withstand the storms of ages." The *American Coast Pilot* disagreed, saying, "A more contemptible light-house does not disgrace Long Island Sound; shamefully erected, and badly kept."

Nineteenth-century view of Black Rock Harbor Lighthouse. *U.S. Coast Guard photo.*

Keeper Stephen Moore's health increasingly failed, and his daughter, Kate, performed all the duties of keeper from a young age. In an interview for the *New York Sunday World* newspaper in 1889, when she was said to be 94, she claimed to have been helping her father from the age of 12. That, however, would have been in 1807, and Stephen Moore didn't become keeper until 1817. Thus it's likely that Kate was actually born in 1805 and was 84 at the time of the interview.

In the 1889 article, Kate was described as having "hazel eyes . . . as bright and her intellect as quick as if she were thirty." She had "ten thousand curious wrinkles," but delicate brown hair with only a few silver ones visible. "She still holds herself erect," wrote the reporter, "although in her daily walk along the shore she generally carries a quaint, knotted staff." Kate described the importance of the light and the difficulties of maintaining the early lamps:

> *Sometimes there were more than two hundred sailing vessels in here at night, and some nights there were as many as three or four wrecks, so you may judge how essential it was that they should see our light.*
>
> *It was a miserable one to keep going, too; nothing like those in use nowadays. It consisted of eight oil lamps which took four gallons of oil each night, and if they were not replenished at stated intervals all through the night, they went out. During windy nights it was impossible to keep them burning at all, and I had to stay there all night, but on other nights I slept at home, dressed in a suit of boys' clothes, my lighted lantern hanging at my headboard and my face turned so that I could see shining on the wall the light from the tower and know if anything happened to it. Our house was forty rods [about 700 feet] from the lighthouse, and to reach it I had to walk across two planks*

under which on stormy nights were four feet of water, and it was not too easy to stay on those slippery, wet boards with the wind whirling and the spray blinding me. I don't want to do it now.

Kate found plenty to keep her busy on the island, as she explained:

I never had much time to get lonely. I had a lot of poultry and two cows to care for, and each year raised twenty sheep, doing the shearing myself, and the killing when necessary. . . .

Then in summer I had my garden to make and keep, for I raised all my own stuff, and, as we had to depend on rain for all the water we used, quite a bit of time was consumed in looking after that. We tried a number of times to dig for water but always struck salt.

You see, I had done all this for so many years, and I knew no other life, so I was sort of fitted for it. I never had much of a childhood as other children have it. That is, I never knew playmates. Mine were the chickens, ducks and lambs and my two Newfoundland dogs.

She also carved and sold duck decoys and had a thriving oyster business. When outsiders trespassed on her oyster beds, Kate would grab her shotgun and tell them, "I represent the United States Government and you've got to go."

Keeper Catherine (Kate) Moore. *Courtesy of Historical Collections, Bridgeport Public Library.*

Keeper Kate was credited with 21 lives saved during her years on the island. "I wish it had been double that number," she said in the *Sunday World* interview.

Of course, there were a great many others, washed up on the shore, half dead, whom we revived, and they all stayed with us until they received means with which to leave. They used to eat up all our provision, and Government never paid us a cent for boarding them.

Although she never went to school, Kate kept a library of around 100 books. She had the rules and regulations for keepers hung on the walls of the house and learned them all by heart. She also had many paintings in the keeper's house, including an original Rubens.

Kate never had the official title of keeper until after her father died at the age of 98 on December 8, 1871. "The sea is a treacherous friend," said Kate, summarizing her life by the ocean. After her 1878 retirement she spent her last years in a cottage with a view of Fayerweather Island.

In an 1838 report, while Stephen Moore was still keeper, Lt. George M. Bache of the U.S. Navy found much to fault at the station. Although the report perceived the light to be very important to local navigation, Bache found that the freestone exterior of the tower was filled in with rubblestone and small pieces of timber. This wood was discovered to be decaying. In addition, the eight lamps and reflectors were "out of proper adjustment," and the light could not be seen at much distance during hazy weather.

Nearly 20 years later the 1856 Annual Report of the Lighthouse Board reported that a new iron lantern and lens apparatus had been installed. A fifth-order Fresnel lens replaced the old system of lamps and reflectors, but the condition of the buildings worsened. The 1868 annual report urged funding for rebuilding the entire station. Nothing substantial was done until 1879, when an attractive new wood-frame keeper's house replaced the "dilapidated old edifice."

Leonard Clark, a Civil War veteran and former whaling captain, replaced Kate Moore and remained keeper for 28 years. Constant pain from a war injury had prompted him to give up whaling for the life of a light keeper. He and his wife raised three children on the island, and one of their sons became keeper of New York's Execution Rocks Lighthouse.

In 1906 Mary Elizabeth Clark became keeper following her husband's death. Two months later John D. Davis, a veteran of the Irish Lighthouse Service, succeeded her. Davis remained until 1932, when two automatic offshore lights replaced the lighthouse.

The lighthouse was given to the city of Bridgeport in 1934. Fayerweather Island became part of Seaside Park, a recreation area established in the nineteenth century largely through the efforts of P. T. Barnum. The historic structure soon fell prey to vandals, who gutted the interior. The 1879 keeper's house was used as a meeting place for community groups until it was destroyed by fire in 1977.

In 1983 the Friends of Seaside Park and the Black Rock Community Council mounted a preservation effort. They replaced the glass and secured the door and windows, and established the island as a nature preserve. Sadly, the lighthouse again became a victim of neglect and vandalism.

Black Rock artist David Grant Grimshaw and caterer Patricia Roche often wondered what could be done to save the lighthouse. As a result of their concern, a lighthouse fund was established in 1993. A Preservation Ball was initiated in 1994 by Grimshaw and became an annual event. With the help of the Black Rock Community Council,

$25,000 worth of cash and in-kind services was raised, and Bridgeport's Board of Park Commissioners matched the amount by granting $25,000.

The Black Rock Seaport Foundation, affiliated with the Black Rock Community Council, oversaw the restoration. Under the direction of architect and Black Rock resident David Barbour, work on the lighthouse proceeded in the spring and summer of 1998. Barbour and landscape architect Stuart Sachs provided in-kind services, and the contractor was American Building Group of Bridgeport.

By the end of the year the masonry was repaired, a coat of graffiti-resistant paint was applied, the lantern room was reglazed, rust on the railings was removed, and new doors and windows were installed. A protective stone seawall was also reconstructed, affording better protection for the foundation. Solar panels were installed in the top of the lighthouse, powering lights that illuminate the tower but don't serve as a navigational aid.

According to an article in the *Bridgeport News*, the lighthouse was temporarily—and mysteriously—relighted in April of 1996. Grimshaw couldn't believe his eyes. "Across the harbor was the eerie glow of the lighthouse against the black sky," he said. Maybe the spirit of Kate Moore had grown tired of waiting for the restoration.

Recent plantings of trees and bushes on the island have helped combat erosion. Deer sometimes forage on the island at night, snowy egrets are seen along the shore, and osprey nest in one of the island's trees. Fayerweather Island and its lighthouse are very much alive.

The island is reached via a mildly strenuous walk across the breakwater that connects it to the end of Barnum Boulevard in Seaside Park in Bridgeport. To reach the park from the east, take I-95 South to Exit 27. Take the "Univ. of Bridgeport/Trans. Center" ramp and stay straight on South Avenue for 0.2 mile. Turn left onto Park Avenue and follow it through the gate to Seaside Park. From the west, take I-95 North to Exit 27. Turn right onto Myrtle Avenue. Turn right onto Railroad Avenue for 0.1 mile, then turn left onto Park Avenue and follow it 0.4 mile through the gate to Seaside Park. There is an admission fee for nonresidents in summer, but a polite request to photograph the lighthouse may be received favorably. Follow Barnum Boulevard to a parking area near a fishing pier and the breakwater leading onto Fayerweather Island. It's about a 20-minute walk to the lighthouse.

To learn more, contact the Fayerweather Island Restoration Fund, c/o Burroughs Community Center, 2470 Fairfield Avenue, Bridgeport, CT 06605, phone (203) 334-0293.

An early twentieth-century postcard showing Bridgeport Harbor Light surrounded by ice. *From the author's collection.*

8

Bridgeport Harbor Light

1851, 1871; destroyed 1953

Bridgeport, the most populous city in Connecticut, grew up around a natural harbor at the mouth of the Pequonnock River. A sandbar at the mouth of the harbor was an obstruction for larger vessels at low tide, however, so the government dredged the channel and built a breakwater in 1844.

Around the same time, Capt. Abraham Archibald McNeil established Bridgeport's first harbor light at his own expense. It consisted of a small, securely anchored boat with a lantern on its mast. A light mounted on multiple piles driven into the harbor bottom replaced the boat a few years later, but by mid-century the federal government was convinced that something better was needed.

On September 28, 1850, Congress appropriated $3,500 for "a beacon light at Bridgeport Harbor." A small iron-pile structure was finished the following year. It was simply a box on four legs topped by an octagonal lantern with a sixth-order lens displaying a fixed red light.

For nearly 20 years Capt. McNeil went back and forth by boat to tend the little light, assisted by his son Charles Hubbell McNeil. But the beacon was plagued by ice in winter, and around 1867 a vessel ran into it and damaged the lantern. The Annual Report of the Lighthouse Board in 1868 presented a case for a new lighthouse.

The request was made a second time—and McNeil given a new boat—before $45,000 was finally appropriated for a new light in July 1870. The new lighthouse was built on a screw-pile foundation about 75 yards from the location of the earlier light, a little under a mile from shore. The structure was similar to a number of lighthouses built in the northeast around 1870, a handsome wood-frame dwelling with a tower mounted at one end of its mansard roof. A fog bell with automatic striking machinery was also installed.

An "icebreaker" around the lighthouse was built by engineer Francis Hopkinson Smith, who was also an artist and writer. The lighthouse was further protected by a granite breakwater that surrounded it. Hundreds of tons of additional riprap stone were added over the years.

The fixed red light was first exhibited from a fourth-order Fresnel lens in November 1871, and the first man in charge was Bridgeport's

The first Bridgeport Harbor Lighthouse, erected in 1851. *From the author's collection.*

longtime keeper Capt. Abraham McNeil. McNeil died in 1873 and was replaced by Waldo Lester. Payroll records indicate that a "Charles Hubbell" was keeper from 1874 to 1875, but it seems likely that this was actually Charles Hubbell McNeil. Charles's brother S. Adolphus McNeil became keeper in 1876 and remained for the next 26 years. Edward Burton served as assistant keeper from 1876 to 1882, when the position was abolished.

During some severe winters the harbor froze over so completely that many people walked to the lighthouse. In 1875 a local couple drove a sleigh from the lighthouse all the way to Fayerweather Island. A newspaper article claimed that in the second half of the bitterly cold February of 1891, throngs of people arrived on foot and by horse.

Despite the protective granite placed around the lighthouse, Keeper Adolphus McNeil nearly had to abandon the building on February 8, 1886, when a large cake of ice hit it and caused $600 worth of damage to the lens. In 1894 the breakwater around the lighthouse was raised and extended 50 feet on the northwest side and a new Gamewell fog bell striking apparatus was installed.

Adolphus McNeil was a single man until 1886, when he married Flora Evans, who had made several long voyages with her sea captain father and was well versed in navigation. She even gave instruction in the art of navigation to some local mariners. An 1887 article in the *Bridgeport Standard* described the McNeils' life at the lighthouse:

> *Mrs. McNeil "paddles her own canoe." . . . She has in her parlor a fine upright piano and a violin resting in a corner of the room invites*

her deft fingers to produce its sweetest tones. On the walls hang several really excellent oil paintings, one of which is an evening view of the harbor showing the lighthouse in the foreground and the steamer Isis *with a schooner in tow. Altogether Capt. McNeil's home is a cozy and desirable one, too quiet perhaps for most people, but he is satisfied that he is in better quarters than he would be in the finest palace on land. He says he remained ashore one or two nights some time ago, but the incessant crowing of the roosters kept him awake and it was a relief to get home again.*

Flora McNeil later reminisced in a 1913 article:

Many a time a wave has dashed into my kitchen window and onto the stove. During the cold weather we used to rub glycerin over the windows to keep the water from freezing on them.

I got used to all kinds of water in those days. Often we would go ashore when you couldn't possibly see either the land or the lighthouse from the boat, only when it was on the crest of a wave. I grew to be quite a sailor and often my husband and I would go out when the water was very rough just for the sport and the experience. We frequently had to sit on opposite sides of the boat to keep it from turning over and when I got back to the house I could wring the water out of my hair I would be so wet. But the experience stood us in good stead when we had to go out in a stormy sea to help other boats in distress.

An unusual addition was made to the station during the stay of the McNeils, in the spring of 1898. Under the authority of the Secretary of the Treasury, a battery of two 10-inch guns was placed on the lighthouse foundation by the War Department to protect the city from perceived dangers during the Spanish-American War.

For a few years Keeper McNeil was given the additional duty of caring for Tongue Point Light at the entrance to the inner harbor. In 1901 he moved ashore to devote himself to that light. After he died in 1904, Flora McNeil became keeper, as detailed in Chapter 9.

Veteran keeper William Hardwick was in charge in December 1920 when the lighter *Calvin Tompkins*, carrying gaskets for the Singer Manufacturing Company in Bridgeport, hit a reef about a mile from Stratford Shoal Lighthouse during a storm. Twelve crewmen were on board. Seven of them evacuated to a rowboat and tried desperately to fight their way through the gale to reach shore.

Keeper Hardwick spotted the boat from the lighthouse and saw that it was foundering. The men had been struggling to stay afloat for

These photos of "Lighthouse Boy" Dan McCoart, Jr., appeared in the *Bridgeport Sunday Post* on May 30, 1937. *Courtesy of the* Connecticut Post.

about four hours, and their boat was breaking apart. The keeper acted quickly, launching the station's boat into heavy seas. He rescued the seven men and brought them back to the lighthouse. "My wife gave them coffee," he later said matter-of-factly. Three other survivors on a raft were rescued by a vessel after about 20 hours, but one died a short time later. Two other crewmen had also died. Hardwick received a letter of commendation from Secretary of Commerce Herbert Hoover.

Providence native Daniel McCoart became keeper in 1921. Two years later he married Elsie Toth, and soon Dan Jr. was born. On June 15, 1930, Keeper McCoart rescued three people whose boat had lost its rudder in a rough sea by towing the vessel into Bridgeport Harbor. Less than two months later, on August 10, a small sailboat capsized near the station with two boys on board. One of the boys couldn't swim and was held up by the other boy until McCoart saved them.

A 1930 article described lighthouse life for the McCoarts. The keeper rowed his son to shore each day and the boy would scramble over the rocks to shore with his lunchbox in hand.

According to the article, every room in the lighthouse was spotless. The entire interior was painted white and green. The living room had a table with a neat pile of magazines, a bookcase with all kinds of literature, a few comfortable chairs, and a stove for heat. There was a radio in the dining room, never used except for the entertainment of guests. In the cellar were two 600-gallon tanks. One stored kerosene for the light, while the other collected rainwater for cooking and washing.

Drinking water came from town in five-gallon bottles, which the keeper picked up by boat. A grocery boy and a milkman would deliver their goods to a specified spot onshore and wave a white handkerchief. At this signal Keeper McCoart would row ashore to fetch the supplies.

Elsie McCoart, described as an excellent cook and baker, kept the pantry well stocked with canned fruits and vegetables and kept the whole place in shipshape condition. "Lonesome? Goodness, I don't have time to be!" she told the reporter.

A 1937 article by Anne Whelan in the *Bridgeport Sunday Post* presented a portrait of Dan Jr., the "Lighthouse Boy." Whelan wrote that Dan "wouldn't give up his home in the harbor, three-quarters of a mile off Seaside Park, for all the farms, the city plots, the baseball diamonds in Bridgeport." Dan's father would sometimes row a friend to the lighthouse to play with his son, and the family's Samoyed dog, Topsy, was an always-ready playmate.

Dan Jr. said there was always something to do: "We always have a good time. We chase one another around the rocks, and we do some fishing, and if we want to play baseball we go to Seaside Park."

Keeper McCoart rowed Dan ashore every morning at 8:00 for his classes at the Sacred Heart School and returned to pick him up at 4:00 p.m. In the winter of 1936–37, Dan missed only three days of school. During more harsh winters he was stuck for days on end at the lighthouse. "There's one thing about this place," he said. "It's fine for homework."

The McCoarts left the lighthouse in 1942, and its operation was eventually taken over by Coast Guard crews. In 1953 plans were announced to replace the lighthouse with a steel skeleton tower. The Coast Guard intended to reassign the four men stationed at the lighthouse and to burn the structure down once the new one was in operation. This plan met with some opposition.

Things looked brighter when the Coast Guard worked out a deal with the Fairfield Dock Company. The firm, citing the lighthouse's historic value, paid $1 for the structure and agreed to pay removal costs of $3,000 to bring it ashore. Then things got darker again.

After much haggling, no agreement could be reached with the mayor of Bridgeport and the Board of Park Commissioners regarding a new location for the lighthouse. With a deadline looming for the building's removal, the owner of the Fairfield Dock Company said the lighthouse would be salvaged for scrap materials.

On December 19, 1953, workers were dismantling the 82-year-old lighthouse when sparks from a bonfire ignited the wooden structure. Workers quickly fled, afraid that the lighthouse's kerosene tank might ignite. People watched from Seaside Park as 50-foot flames engulfed the building. Within an hour only the twisted foundation remained, and a vital part of local history and culture was consigned to memory. The following spring a new, decidedly homely steel tower was completed.

CHAPTER 9

Tongue Point Light in 2002. *Photo by the author.*

Tongue Point Light

(Bridgeport Breakwater Light, Bug Light)
1895

From early shipbuilding and whaling to manufacturing and coastal trade, Bridgeport owed its development to a large harbor at the mouth of the Pequonnock River on Long Island Sound. Today Bridgeport Harbor is one of only three deepwater ports in Connecticut.

In 1891, the same year the city's favorite son P. T. Barnum died, a breakwater was built at Tongue Point at the west side of the entrance to the inner harbor, providing a harbor of refuge. In 1893 and 1894 federal appropriations totaling $4,500 were secured for the installation of a lighthouse at the end of this breakwater, extending out from Tongue Point (also known as Wells Point) about 500 feet from shore.

The tower, constructed under the supervision of Lt. Col. D. P. Heap of the Lighthouse Board, is a smaller example of the numerous prefabricated cast-iron lighthouses erected between the 1870s and early 1900s. The 31-foot tower (22 feet to the base of the lantern deck) is about 12 feet in diameter at its base. A spiral stairway leads from the base to the watchroom, and from there a ladder reaches into the octagonal iron lantern. Unlike most similar towers, Tongue Point Light is not lined with brick.

On March 1, 1895, the sixth-order Fresnel lens was lighted for the first time, replacing a temporary lantern used since the beginning of the previous year. A keeper's dwelling was never erected, as the authorities apparently thought the lighthouse was close enough to shore to make a resident keeper an unnecessary expense. It was first put under the charge of the longtime keeper of Bridgeport Harbor Lighthouse, S. Adolphus McNeil. McNeil's father had established the first light in Bridgeport Harbor, and his brother John was harbormaster at the time Tongue Point Lighthouse came into being.

After a $1,200 appropriation in 1897, an electrically operated "fog gong" was established at the station. This apparatus proved unreliable and was replaced in 1899 by a 160-pound bell mounted on the side of the tower, along with a new clockwork-operated striking mechanism.

Shortly after the turn of the century, Keeper McNeil gave up his duties as keeper of Bridgeport Harbor Light, moving to shore and concentrating on the light at Tongue Point. Tending the little light on the breakwater was easy enough in fair weather, but walking out on the breakwater or reaching the station by boat could be hair-raising in heavy seas or fog, in spite of the addition of a landing wharf in 1896 and a plank walkway on the breakwater in 1900.

The 1905 Annual Report of the Lighthouse Board noted that the keeper had "erected at his own expense a small shanty in which he sleeps nightly that he may be ready to start the fog-signal machinery at shortest notice." Despite recommendations to buy land and build a dwelling, no appropriation was ever made and no keeper's house ever constructed. Even if it had been built, it would have been too late for S. Adolphus McNeil, who died in December 1904 and was replaced by his widow, Flora Evans McNeil, at a salary of $300 per year. "When he died I asked for it," she was quoted as saying in a newspaper article, "and although they were already giving up the idea of allowing women to become lighthouse keepers they knew that I had actually been the keeper of the light for 20 years and I was allowed to retain it without even an examination."

As a young girl, Flora had accompanied her sea captain father, John Evans, to South America and mastered the art of navigation at his side. Described in a newspaper article as "a woman of attractive personality, a successful business manager, an interesting conversationalist and an aspirant for the vote," Mrs. McNeil earned much respect during her years as a light keeper and businesswoman.

A 1913 article described Flora McNeil bundled in a rubber coat, hat, and high rubber boats, scurrying along the plank walkway on the breakwater to reach the lighthouse through high wind and rain. She downplayed the hazards of the job:

> *As a rule, there is nothing really interesting about the work. Of course, during a heavy storm it isn't exactly fun to take a trip out to the lighthouse, but the light must be going and the worse the weather the more necessary for it to be going. . . . Usually it is simply a matter of going out at sunrise to turn off the light and at sunset to light it. If there is a storm or a fog the bell, too, must be turned on. I have gone out in the middle of the night to start the fog bell, but as a rule I have had someone go with me.*

The work, however, could be dangerous at times, according to Flora:

> *I think perhaps the hardest trips are the ones made in winter when it has rained and turned cold for the plank is then a glare of ice and naturally very slippery. I have been out during snowstorms*

when the plank was so slippery it was scarcely possible to keep your footing and when the storm was so heavy that all you could see in front of you was the falling snow. You could hear the roar of water under your feet and see the snow melt as it touched the waves but you could hardly more than guess where to put your next step.

Flora McNeil lived at 61 Lafayette Street in Bridgeport. She ran a manicure business in the Meigs Building, practically leading a double life as a well-dressed businesswoman by day, dedicated light keeper in her off hours. An expert boater, Flora claimed the sea never frightened her.

It isn't exactly a pleasure to take a trip out there when a fog is coming on or when a heavy snow is falling with it so dark you can hardly see your hand before your face. You can hear the moaning water on either side of you and if you were on some desert island you could not feel more alone and forsaken by all humanity. There is not a sign of human life, the wind whistles and moans, the waters lap the rocks wildly and the rain beats into your face.

I suppose some people would think it an impossible thing to do—and probably it would be impossible for them—but I am almost as much at home on or in the water as I am on land and I have no real fear of the water even when it is angry.

Early twentieth-century postcard showing the steamer *Park City* passing Tongue Point Light. *From the author's collection.*

Coast Guard Electrician's Mate 1st Class Carl Golden at Tongue Point Light during a semiannual inspection of lighthouse optics in the area. *U.S. Coast Guard photo.*

The breakwater at Tongue Point was never popular with the captains of large vessels, who complained about the sharp turn they had to make as they rounded the breakwater to enter the inner harbor. In 1919 the situation was remedied by the removal of 350 feet of the breakwater. The granite that was removed was added to the tops of two breakwaters at each side of the entrance to the harbor. When the breakwater was shortened, a derrick was used to move the lighthouse onto a 10-foot-high concrete foundation at its present position, 275 feet closer to shore. The harbor was dredged and widened around the same time.

The light was automated in 1954. In September of that year, attendant Robert Baker was checking the light at about 10:30 p.m. as a major hurricane approached the coast. He was surprised to see a man fishing from a rock about 20 feet from the lighthouse. The man hadn't noticed that the incoming storm tide had cut off his access back to shore. Baker called the police, who swiftly arrived in a boat to take the 39-year-old man off the rock. It was reported that he had two small fish and an eel to show for his risky efforts.

The Coast Guard proposed discontinuing the light and fog signal in 1967, but local protests saved "Bug Light," as it's known locally. Today the solar-powered light, flashing green every four seconds, continues as an aid to navigation. The sixth-order lens has been replaced with a modern optic and there is no longer a fog signal.

A 1985 survey showed that the old fog bell, although no longer used, was still at the lighthouse. The striking mechanism for the bell was also still there, as were 15 weights associated with the machine. By 1989 these items had been removed.

On June 4, 2004, it was announced that the Coast Guard had determined the lighthouse to be excess federal property and that it would be made available to an eligible entity pursuant to the National

Undated Coast Guard photo of Tongue Point Light. The fog bell was still in place next to the lighthouse when the photo was taken.

Historic Lighthouse Preservation Act of 2000. But a few months later the potential transfer of Tongue Point Lighthouse was put on indefinite hold because of issues of access. The lighthouse is adjacent to the grounds of the Bridgeport Harbor Generating Station and the only land access is across that property.

It's hard to get a good view of this lighthouse from land. An excellent vantage point is readily available from the decks of the Bridgeport-to-Port Jefferson ferry, which passes very close to the lighthouse as it leaves and enters the harbor.

CHAPTER 10

Stratford Shoal Light in 2002. *Photo by the author.*

Stratford Shoal Light

(Middleground Light)
1877

Stratford Shoal Light has often been categorized as a New York lighthouse, but according to U.S. Geological Survey maps it's clearly on the Connecticut side of Long Island Sound by about 1,000 feet. It's perhaps best to think of Stratford Shoal Light simply as a Long Island Sound lighthouse rather than as a possession of either state. For the purposes of this volume, it belongs in Connecticut.

Beginning around 1820, Middleground Shoal, about three-quarters of a mile in length, was marked by two spar buoys to the north and south. In March 1837 an appropriation of $10,000 made possible a small lightship (built at Norfolk, Virginia) that was placed off the southeastern extremity of the shoal by the following January. A report by Lt. George M. Bache made in November of 1838 provides a description:

> *This light-boat is a vessel of about 100 tons burden, under the charge of a captain and mate, and manned by a crew of four men; ample provision appears to have been made for the accommodation of the crew, and for the stowage of wood and water for four-months' supply, and of oil for one year. The lights are shown from two masts, which are fitted for the purpose—one 40 feet, the other 50 feet in height; each lantern contains a compass-lamp, which is fitted to burn ten wicks. This vessel appears to be well calculated for the station she occupies; it must be observed, however, that, in consequence of being made to ride to a single anchor of 1,200 pounds weight, when first placed there, she has been driven several times from her proper position.*

The 73-foot light vessel was called Stratford Point Light Vessel or Stratford Shoal Light Vessel until it was designated LV-15 in 1867. It was dragged from its position several more times over the years, usually by drifting ice. In 1875 it was "in poor condition" after being dragged out of position by ice and subsequently towed to New London. It broke free again early the next year and was eventually found near Faulkner's Island, about 23 miles to the northeast.

Meanwhile, $50,000 had been appropriated on March 3, 1873, for a lighthouse to replace the LV-15. Two more appropriations of $50,000 each were needed to complete the project.

Stratford Shoal Lighthouse was planned during the early part of the era when most offshore lighthouses were built on tubular cast-iron foundations. The final plan in this location, however, called for a granite dwelling-and-lighthouse combination atop a cylindrical granite-and-concrete pier. Lighthouse Service engineer Edward L. Woodruff was credited with the design. During 18 years as superintendent of construction in the Third Lighthouse District, Woodruff also designed New York's Race Rock and Stepping Stones lighthouses.

Work began in 1874 with the laying of a ring of granite riprap at the site. The contract for the pier came too late for work to progress that year, and over the winter much gravel from the shoal was swept into the granite ring. When work commenced in 1875, the contractor had to first clear out the gravel before concrete could be laid and the first courses of the pier put into place. The project moved slowly but steadily forward. In 1876 the Annual Report of the Lighthouse Board reported that

> *the first course of the cutstone pier and the concrete backing were completed, and several cargoes of riprap-stone delivered at the work in places where the former riprap had settled in consequence of the scouring out of the gravel-bed. This scour occurs at the stage of low water and during the prevalence of gales. The third course of the pier and thirty-four stones of the fourth course have been completed and put in place during this season.*

The granite pier, including a cellar and cisterns, was completed by December 1, 1876. The pier is 55 feet in diameter at its base, tapering to 46 feet at the top. During the following spring the surface of the pier was leveled and a temporary wharf was added for landing materials for the lighthouse. The walls of the lighthouse were begun in the summer of 1877, but the building couldn't be completed that year. Another setback was described in the annual report of 1878. In November 1877 the construction schooner *Mignonette* broke loose from its moorings, struck the rocks, and sank. The crew escaped injury and most of the materials were salvaged, and work progressed.

The dwelling is 28 feet on a side, with walls about 18 inches thick. The 35-foot tower is lined with brick and projects five feet out from the dwelling's south façade. Inside the tower, which is octagonal above the second story, a spiral stairway climbs to the upper levels. The design of the lighthouse is very similar to that of Race Rock Light in Fisher's Island Sound, but the two have different roof shapes and window arches. According to the listing in the National Register of

Historic Places, "Stratford Shoal exhibits some Gothic Revival details, such as pointed windows on the third story of the tower. . . . The Gothic detail and tall tower lend an institutional air to the lighthouse, saved from an ecclesiastical reference by the tower's position on the façade rather than at the gable end."

A fourth-order Fresnel lens was installed and a flashing white light was first exhibited from 60 feet above the water on December 15, 1877.

The first keeper of Stratford Shoal Light was William McGloin, originally from Ireland, who had been the captain of the LV-15 lightship since early the previous year. (After the lighthouse went into service, the little lightship was sold and later used as a floating barracks during construction of New York's Great Beds Lighthouse.)

McGloin remained keeper until 1880. The lighthouse had a head keeper and two assistants, with plenty of turnover, as might be expected at an isolated, waveswept location. Ezra Mott arrived as second assistant in 1881, progressed to first assistant two years later, then became head keeper in 1885. Mott's wife and children lived ashore.

A newspaper article stressed the isolation of the station. Mott and the two assistants always enjoyed hearing news from shore, and newspapers were highly valued. It was said, in fact, that parties fishing around the shoal always had better luck when they brought along a bundle of newspapers for the keepers.

On Monday, March 14, 1887, an assistant keeper named John P. Hutchinson Jr. left Port Jefferson on Long Island to row back to the lighthouse. Days went by with no sign of Hutchinson. That Friday the *New York Times* reported that the boat and Hutchinson's hat had drifted ashore, and it was apparent that he had drowned.

Gilbert L. Rulon became head keeper in September 1901. In August 1905 Rulon was ashore on vacation when the most bizarre drama in the lighthouse's history played itself out. Left in charge was First Assistant Keeper Morrell Hulse, a 54-year-old Long Island native and former packet sailor who had just served two years as an assistant keeper at Rhode Island's Whale Rock Light. Also at the lighthouse was Second Assistant Keeper Julius Koster of New York City, a newcomer to the Lighthouse Service.

According to newspaper reports, Hulse was taken by complete surprise when Koster charged at him with a razor lashed to the end of a pole. Hulse fought off Koster, who seemed to calm down for the moment. But similar scenes took place over the next couple of days, forcing Hulse to stay awake night and day. He not only had to defend himself against the deranged Koster but also had to make sure the

Morrell Edson Hulse was a key player in a 1905 drama at Stratford Shoal Light. *Photo courtesy of Long Island Genealogy, www.longislandgenealogy.com.*

light continued to function properly.

One afternoon Hulse found Koster chopping at the lighthouse walls with a hammer and chisel. Later that night Hulse became aware that the light had stopped revolving. Rushing to the lantern room, he found Koster holding an axe and about to destroy the lens. It isn't clear whether Hulse used brute force, gentle persuasion, or both, but he somehow dissuaded Koster from his violent intent.

According to the *Washington Post*, Hulse didn't get a moment's sleep or rest for the next five days as he protected himself and the light. Koster eventually turned his rage on himself and threatened suicide. When help finally arrived, Koster was found with self-inflicted gashes on his neck and was taken to a hospital. During the following year, Hulse was awarded a Diploma of Honor by La Société des Sauveteurs for his courageous defense of the lighthouse. The French organization bestowed the honor because it was said that Hulse's actions had prevented the possible loss of a French vessel in the vicinity.

In *Lighthouse Mysteries of the North Atlantic*, Robert Ellis Cahill writes that Julius Koster returned to his New York City home and soon succeeded at committing suicide. According to Cahill, later keepers experienced disturbances at the lighthouse that they blamed on a ghost they called Julius. The reported phenomena included doors slamming themselves, chairs thrown against walls, and pans of hot water thrown from the stove.

Rescues in the vicinity of the lighthouse were not uncommon. On August 18, 1911, the keepers witnessed a sailboat capsize in heavy seas as its three-man crew tried to reach Port Jefferson from Bridgeport. Two assistant keepers, John H. Paul and Nicholas Sarre, started for the scene in the station's rowboat. The sailboat was two and a half miles from the lighthouse, and it took a full five hours for the keepers to reach the three men on the sailboat and get them safely to land. Both men received lifesaving medals for their heroism.

Keeper Emil Usinger was credited with saving five people from a disabled boat during a storm in 1915. And on July 27, 1930, First Assistant Keeper John A. Tatay saved the life of a swimmer by lowering a boat and rushing to the man's aid as he was being carried away by a strong ebb tide. The man had been part of a fishing party anchored near the lighthouse.

In December 1919 two assistant keepers had to rescue themselves. William Prumuka and Harold Hobson, both natives of Bridgeport, were headed to shore from the lighthouse when a rope became entangled in the propeller in rough seas. This put the motor out of commission, and the men drifted helplessly through the afternoon and a frigid night, a total of almost 20 hours. The next morning they made it to Port Jefferson, Long Island. It was reported that Prumuka's hands and Hobson's feet were frozen. After two weeks of medical care, the men went to Bridgeport and eventually got a boat ride back to the lighthouse.

Lewis J. Allen of Norwalk became keeper in 1928, and on one occasion saved the lives of two Bridgeport girls who were unable to control their canoe in heavy seas. Keeper Allen, a Spanish-American War veteran and longtime sailor, was involved in an even more dramatic rescue about two years later.

Late at night on Wednesday, February 8, 1933, the 30-foot powerboat *Saugatuck* left Westport, Connecticut, to search for a teenager named Eddie Connelly, who had not returned from a clam-digging expedition in a rowboat. On board were Capt. John Mulhaley, the mother of Eddie Connelly, Mulhaley's wife and 18-year-old daughter, and nine other men. Three men disembarked at Cockenoe Island to look for Connelly.

Off Cockenoe Island, the *Saugatuck* became disabled with a broken tiller and then a dead motor and began to drift eastward with the other 10 people still on board. One of the men, police sergeant Howard Baker, took charge along with another man after Mulhaley collapsed early Thursday morning. Baker spent long periods lying flat on his stomach at the stern, using a long plank in an effort to steer the boat to shore.

Through the entire night and all of Thursday the boat continued drifting to the east until, late at night, they saw Penfield Reef Lighthouse off Fairfield. Friday dawned and they continued drifting past Bridgeport Harbor. Search planes combed the sound but failed to spot

Stratford Shoal Light, circa 1960s. *U.S. Coast Guard photo.*

the *Saugatuck*. A red sweater was hung from a mast and the passengers tried frantically to signal passing vessels for help, but none stopped. By 10:00 a.m. they could see Stratford Shoal Lighthouse. At noon the freezing and desperately hungry group set a drum of gasoline on fire and set it adrift, hoping to attract the attention of the keepers.

Keeper Allen and Assistant Keeper Alfred Auger saw the burning gasoline and quickly responded. They had to chop a heavy coating of ice from the launching gear for the station's powerboat, but they managed to reach the *Saugatuck* and tow it to the lighthouse in heavy seas. The 10 people on board had been adrift without food or water for about 38 hours. Mulhaley's hands were badly frostbitten and were said to be twice their normal size.

After a few hours at the lighthouse, word came by radio that Eddie Connelly had spent Wednesday night at Peck's Ledge Lighthouse. On Thursday he and the three men on Cockenoe Island were picked up by a boat from Norwalk and taken to safety. "God was good to us," said Connelly's mother. A couple of weeks later, Keepers Allen and Auger were commended for their heroism by Secretary of Commerce Roy Chapin.

Under the Coast Guard, four or five men were assigned to Stratford Shoal Light, with each of them on duty for two weeks followed by one week off. The year 1955 was a memorable one at the station. On

February 1, 1955, two Coast Guard keepers stationed at the light, Harry Buede and Jerry Hill, were coming into Bridgeport in a 20-foot boat when they struck ice and developed a leak. They got the boat safely to a municipal dock. Three months later, on May 5, the 10,000-ton tanker *Menara* went aground about a mile northeast of the lighthouse, thankfully with no major damage or casualties.

On June 23 of that same year a test pilot named Lyle Monkton had to parachute from his F-84 Thunderstreak fighter plane after its engine failed at 25,000 feet. He landed not far from the lighthouse and was quickly picked up by a family out fishing. Moments later two of the Coast Guard light keepers, Harry Buede and William Schumacher, arrived in their motor launch. The unscathed Monkton told his rescuers, "First swim I've had this year."

In addition to the stories of the resident ghost known as Julius, the shoal itself has its otherworldly legend. It's said that back in the early nineteenth century a ship called the *Trustful* was about to leave Bridgeport with a cargo of church bells. The weather was stormy and the seas grew rough, but the captain insisted on sailing. He told those in favor of staying ashore, "The *Trustful* will be all right. The devil looks after his own. Anyway, if we do go down, these bells here will never ring in Setauket, but they may peal a dirge for some of you white-livered folk at the bottom of the sea."

According to the legend, the *Trustful* went to the bottom of the sea near Middleground Shoal, and not a trace of ship or crew was ever found. But it's said that if you listen closely as you sail the sound near Middleground Shoal, you can hear the eerie clang of muffled church bells emanating from the sea bottom. The *Trustful* is also said to appear as a ghost ship in full sail off the shoal.

The lighthouse was automated in the summer of 1970, and the four Coast Guard crewmen were reassigned. A contractor hired by the Coast Guard performed some renovation, including repointing of the granite masonry, in the mid-1980s. Today the modern VRB-25 optic continues to flash white every five seconds. In 2004 the Coast Guard installed a new solar array and automatic monitoring system.

This lighthouse can be seen distantly (bring binoculars and a telephoto lens) from the Bridgeport-to-Port Jefferson ferry. To get closer you'll need to be in a private boat or charter.

CHAPTER 11

Stratford Point Light in October 2004. *Photo by the author.*

11

Stratford Point Light

1821, 1881

According to legend, many years before a lighthouse was built at Stratford Point a vessel was passing close by on its way to New Amsterdam as the wind blew a gale and the seas grew heavy. The captain was aware of a nearby point of land extending into Long Island Sound, but in the thick weather he couldn't see how close it was. He ordered his crew to their knees, and they all prayed for salvation.

A short time later the men saw a great tongue of flame illuminating the shore and guiding them away from danger. They hailed the flame as a "miracle light," and thus the land we now call Stratford Point was long known as Miracle Point.

Jutting far into the sound at the western side of the entrance to the Housatonic River, Stratford Point was a dangerous obstacle for coastal shipping traffic and for vessels entering the river. Miracle lights aside, tradition tells us that local citizens displayed a bonfire on the point, which was later replaced by a signal fire on a pole. Something more permanent was in order and on March 3, 1821, Congress appropriated $4,000 for a lighthouse and keeper's dwelling. A short time later two acres of land for the station was purchased from Betsy Walker.

The first lighthouse at Stratford Point was very similar to the one built earlier at Five Mile Point in New Haven. It was an octagonal wooden tower 28 feet high, with sides alternately painted black and white. The keeper's house was a plain affair, a wood-frame one-and-a-half-story cottage, 26 by 27 feet, close to the lighthouse tower. It had two small bedrooms, a kitchen, and a parlor on the first floor, and a single bedroom upstairs.

The buildings were only partially built when a tremendous storm swept through the area. The framework of the Stratford Point tower survived, a tribute to contractor Judson Curtis and the hardy timbers used in those days.

The first keeper was Samuel Buddington, who raised seven children with his wife, Amy, at the station. Members of the Buddington family kept the light for nearly a half century, except for a three-year period when Samuel was replaced for not being a member of the correct political party.

An 1837 inspection wasn't kind to Keeper Buddington, reporting the lighthouse to be "in the worst order imaginable." Oil was dripping from the lantern to the base of the tower through holes in the lantern deck floor. "There are the strongest indications of this lighthouse being kept in the most careless, and slovenly manner," continued the report.

A report made the following year by Lt. George M. Bache was less harsh but still critical. The five-room dwelling was reported to be in good order. The tower was undergoing repairs, possibly to shore up the holes in the lantern room floor. Bache wrote:

> *The lighting apparatus consists of ten lamps, with parabolic reflectors, arranged in two clusters . . . the axes of the reflectors, at the extremities of each cluster, diverge from each other 43°, and each light is placed a little without the focus of its reflector, which causes a slight convergence in the beam of reflected light. . . .*
>
> *The machinery for producing the revolution of the lights . . . caused a half revolution of the tables every two minutes; its proper rate being 2'15". The light-keeper has no means of judging accurately of its rate. . . . The keeper informed me that it stopped last January, owing to dust having collected in parts of it, when it was taken apart and cleaned; it stopped once, also, in the summer of 1838.*

Samuel Buddington died in 1848 and his wife, Amy, was appointed as his replacement. Judging by an 1850 inspection report, Amy may

Stratford Point Light, circa 1870s. *National Archives photo.*

have been a more efficient keeper than her late husband, and her son Rufus acted as an unofficial assistant. The 1850 report found the lighthouse and dwelling in good order.

A new lighting apparatus consisting of six Argand lamps and 21-inch reflectors was installed in 1855. By 1859 that equipment was replaced by a fifth-order Fresnel lens, which was in turn replaced a few years later by a third-order lens. That would eventually be replaced by a smaller, fourth-order lens in 1932. A fog bell and striking machinery were added in 1864.

Rufus Buddington, who had a wife and six children of his own, succeeded his mother as keeper in 1861. The Buddington era came to an end in 1869, when Benedict Lillingston arrived with his wife, Marilla. Keeper Lillingston's son, Frederick, who was also a talented artist, served as assistant. The keeper's young granddaughter, Charlotte (Lottie), lived at the station after her mother died. Lottie looked after a flock of Spanish hens, gathered blackberries and beach plums for jam, helped tend the vegetable garden, and gathered seashells on the shore. Her uncle Frederick served as a teacher and her grandfather, Benedict, taught her how to make fishing nets.

The two keepers were never absent from the station at the same time—never, that is, except during an October night in 1871 when a terrific gale pounded the light station. Keeper Lillingston burst into the living room and told Frederick that he had sighted a vessel in distress. "'Twill take both of us, in this gale, to be of any help," he shouted, according to a newspaper account. "Lottie must take care of the light." The two men rushed out into the night, leaving little Lottie alone with her grandmother Marilla, who lay ill upstairs.

Lottie knew that the steamer *Elm City* was due to pass the lighthouse at 11:00. At about 10:30 she decided to check the light. She passed from the house through the passageway to the tower and carefully ascended the stairs; at the top she saw that the light was out.

Thinking quickly, Lottie returned to the house and fetched a small brass lantern, lit it, and carried it up into the tower. She stopped the clockwork mechanism that turned the lens, put the lantern inside the lens, and then started the mechanism again.

"Stratford Light dim for half hour last night" was the report made later by the captain of the *Elm City*. But the dim light, thanks to Lottie, guided the steamer past the point.

Much later in her life, Lottie wrote a brief history of the light station. She recalled that vegetables were grown in a garden, and that meat and groceries were obtained from the village four miles away. And although she claimed that the lighthouse in the early 1870s "was nearly as pristine as when it was first established by the government," Lighthouse Board reports during that period don't agree. The 1867 report, for example, stated:

> *The tower is of wood and shows signs of decay. The lantern, of an inferior model, rests on a brick parapet, and is constantly out of repair and leaky. The lighting apparatus . . . gives flashes too short in duration and at intervals too long. The tower should be rebuilt and provided with suitable oil and store-rooms. The keeper's dwelling is in tolerable condition as yet, but rather small for a station with an assistant. It would therefore seem expedient to rebuild it at the same time as the tower. The fog-bell is of little or no use, and a more efficient one should take the place of it as soon as practicable.*

The next year's report made the situation sound even more dire:

> *This station is in bad condition. The tower is of wood, shingled outside, but without ceiling or lining inside; it is old, leaks badly, and is very frail; the lantern is too small.*

In 1869 and 1870 requests were made for $50,000 for new buildings. The request was downgraded to $15,000 in 1871 and 1872, when the annual report said the buildings were "very old and unfit for occupation." These pleas were repeated in 1873 and 1874, but for some reason the matter was then dropped until 1879, when the dwelling and tower were described as "dilapidated" and a modest request for $10,000 was made.

Because the dwelling was too small for a keeper, an assistant, and their families, the government helped stave off the inevitable rebuilding by assigning married couples to the station. John L. Brush replaced Benedict Lillingston as keeper at $560 per year in 1874, and Brush's wife, Abigail, served as his assistant for $425 yearly. Another husband and wife, Jerome and Mary Tuttle, were keeper and assistant from 1879 to 1880.

Funding was finally secured for the rebuilding of the station in 1880, and construction was finished the following year. The new 35-foot tower was constructed of five courses of cast-iron plates, a design largely credited to Lighthouse Board engineer Gen. James Chatham Duane. A number of similar towers were constructed, mainly in New England, from the 1870s to the 1890s. The cast-iron shell was lined with brick. A cast-iron spiral stairway led to the watchroom level, and from there a ladder led to the octagonal lantern room. The familiar brown band around the conical white tower was added on May 15, 1899.

A new wood-frame keeper's house was built about 45 feet north of the tower. This house originally had eight rooms, including three bedrooms, a dining room, kitchen, sitting room, and pantry. A new fog bell tower was also constructed about 20 feet southwest of the lighthouse.

The rotating third-order Fresnel lens in use at this time was manufactured by L. Sautter of Paris.The Henry-Lepaute clockwork mechanism needed to be wound every four hours to keep the lens revolving.

Stratford native Theodore Judson became keeper shortly before the rebuilding of the house and tower. The Judson family lived in the old house for a year before the new one was ready. The old house was left standing and gradually fell apart. It was still standing as late as 1918.

Judson's wife, Kate, served as assistant until after the station was rebuilt, when the position was abolished. After that, an official assistant wasn't assigned to the station until after 1910. "Theed" Judson remained keeper at Stratford Point for over 40 years, and the Judsons were mostly well respected. But there were the occasional odd stories from Stratford Point that earned the keeper the nickname "Crazy" Judson. It was a name not given lightly.

A headline in the *Newark Daily Advocate* in late July 1886 read, "A Big Sea Serpent." The paper went on to report the following:

> *A sea serpent with pea green whiskers passed down Long Island Sound in a big hurry Wednesday morning. He was plowing through the water at a 25 knot clip when he passed the Stratford lighthouse and left a wake of foam behind him a mile in length. He was easily 200 feet in length, and his head was reared 20 feet above the brine. That afforded a good look at his whiskers, which were the rich deep green color of bog hay.*
>
> *The big reptile was plainly seen from the lighthouse by Keeper Theodore Judson, his wife, his son Henry and his daughter Agnes, and by H. W. Curtis of Stratford, as well as by a number of people at Captain John Bond's place up the river. These latter saw only the loftily reared head, which at a distance looked like the tail funnel of a sound flier. Keeper Judson seriously declared to a reporter that he could not be mistaken.*
>
> *The other witnesses all corroborate Keeper Judson's statement, which bears the imprint of truth. Incumbency in the lighthouse service is prima facie evidence of sobriety, an element not always closely connected with stories of sea monsters.*
>
> *Still the pea green whiskers are inexplicable.*

This report came a decade before the May 1896 sighting of a 300-foot sea serpent by Keeper John Skipworth at Saybrook Breakwater

Light (see Chapter 17 for details). It seems that there was either a contagious hysteria on Long Island Sound in the late nineteenth century, or possibly a sly conspiracy of lighthouse keepers having a little fun by tweaking the press.

There were other reported sightings in Long Island Sound in that period, some possibly sparked by P. T. Barnum's offer in 1873 of $50,000 to anyone who could produce a sea serpent carcass. But Barnum died in 1891, so that probably wasn't a motivation for Skipworth.

It was a July 1915 interview that earned Judson the "crazy" label for eternity. Barnum had also once offered $20,000 for a captured mermaid, but that was many years earlier and wouldn't seem to have had any bearing on Judson's next strange sighting. Here's what Judson told a reporter in 1915:

> *Three days ago, I saw a shoal of mermaids off Lighthouse point. I've seen them again and again, but it's only once I laid hands on one. She scratched me well, but I got her brush away from her and I've got it yet. It's generally in the early morning or late afternoon that they gather around the rocks off the point. Sometimes I've counted as many as 12 or 15 of them, their yellow hair glistening and their scaly tails flashing. They're a grand sight.*
>
> *It was late afternoon when I happened to be out there alone. The sky was thickening for a storm and a fog was creeping up and I had just set the foghorn going. It seems to have an attraction for mermaids, just as the light has for moths. But all of a sudden I noticed this one sitting here all by herself, combing her long golden hair. I took a long look at her before I crept up to her and it's just as well I did, else I wouldn't be able to give you much of a description, everything happened so quick once I touched her. . . . She had lovely gazelle eyes and a fair skin. She was just like a woman to her waist and below that all silver-spangled scales. I should say her tail was about three feet long. The upper part of her body was a little smaller than the average woman. I should say she weighed, all told, about 75 pounds. . . . To tell you the truth, I was hesitating in my own mind when I went out for her whether I would keep her for myself and let the $20,000 go—she was so beautiful!*
>
> *The mermaid didn't scream or squeak but she had a tongue and beautiful white teeth. The only sound she made was a hissing noise and it matched well to her temper.*

The mermaid regrettably escaped when the keeper tried to grab her. Asked if he had ever tried to lasso a mermaid, Judson answered,

"Might as well try to lasso an eel." But for anyone who was interested, the keeper was happy to produce the mermaid's hairbrush. He explained that mermaids took brushes and combs from the staterooms of wrecked steamers, accounting for the ordinary, cheap look of the brush. The entire fishy tale was supported by Kate Judson and Assistant Keeper Will Petzolt.

A year later, in July 1916, the following brief item made the papers:

> *LIGHTHOUSE KEEPER SIGHTS A SUBMARINE*
> *Theodore Judson, keeper of the Stratford lighthouse, reported sighting at 6:45 a.m. a large submarine bound east. The vessel is larger than the United States navy submarines, he says.*

There was no word on whether anyone believed Judson, but in any case the submarine did not fire any salvos at Stratford. Crazy or not, Judson was regarded as a highly competent worker. "It is a true saying that when a keeper's light goes out, he can consider himself out of a job," he said in 1918.

Keeper "Theed" Judson, left, was head keeper at Stratford Point from 1880 to 1921. Will Petzolt served as Judson's assistant and was then head keeper from 1921 to 1945. *Courtesy of Stratford Historical Society.*

Once in a snowy February the fog bell at the station had to be rung continuously for 104 hours, followed by a four-hour break and then another 103 hours of sounding. The clockwork mechanism for the bell had to be wound every two and a half hours, and each winding took about 20 minutes. In 1911 a new first-class fog siren replaced the fog bell, with air compressors and diesel engines housed in a new brick building west of the lighthouse. During Judson's stay the siren once had to be run for 54 consecutive hours.

Agnes Judson, the keeper's daughter, gained fame as a swimmer and won competitions in the area. One July day in 1897, when she was 17, Agnes watched from the lighthouse as the seas became increasingly rough. Two fishermen about 100 yards offshore were trying to pull up the anchor of their small yawl, and the waves caused both to fall into the sea.

Agnes ran down the lighthouse stairs. She called to her brother, Henry, and both swam out to the fishermen. One of them was about to go under a second time when Agnes got a rope to him. Agnes and Henry managed to pull both of the men safely back to shore. When asked how she had summoned so much courage, Agnes replied, "Why, I couldn't stand by and see those two poor fellows drown, could I? I just jumped in and helped them—same as anyone would have done who knows how to swim."

Keeper Judson retired in 1921. At the time he claimed that he hadn't had a vacation in 39 years. When he died at 87 in 1935, the *New York Times* called Judson a "picturesque character" and, in an understatement, "a raconteur of salty tales." It was said that friends never got him to retract his mermaid story.

Will Petzolt, who had been assistant keeper since 1913, replaced Judson. Petzolt was involved in at least two rescues during his years at Stratford Point. In 1918 as assistant he saved two boys on a disabled boat, and in 1922 he and his assistant rescued 30 passengers from the stranded power vessel *Ellen May*. Petzolt remained keeper at Stratford Point until 1945.

Another colorful keeper at Stratford Point was Daniel McCoart of Providence, Rhode Island, who arrived in 1945. He had been keeper of Bridgeport Harbor Lighthouse for over 20 years. McCoart was a navy veteran and former boxer, a no-nonsense tough guy who snorted at sea serpents and gave mermaids the brush-off, according to a newspaper profile. "A look from Cap'n Dan," said the article, "is nothing trivial. In a lion's den it would wreck the appetites of assailants at ten feet."

"You know," McCoart told the reporter, "lots of people think we have nothing to do out here but sit on our beam-ends and whittle like those hermits you hear about." For the dedicated McCoart and his assistant, William Shackley, this was far from the truth.

McCoart declared that the best thing about lighthouse work was not having a nagging boss on your back, and the worst thing was what he called "lighthouse promises." He explained that while keeper in Bridgeport Harbor he had rescued many people who always promised him the world for saving their lives. "Then they go home," he said, "and you never hear a squeak out of them."

In the late 1940s artist William McCracken lived close to the light station with his family. His daughter, Indiana graphic designer Peg Caudell, recalls that Assistant Keeper Shackley was a great friend to her and her family. "He let my two sisters and me go up and help him light the lighthouse on our birthdays," says Caudell. "It was so exciting, climbing the stairs and then that ladder to the light. . . . He was a wonderful person and his wife Esther was as well."

McCoart retired as the light's last civilian keeper in 1963. His career spanned 45 years, including 18 at Stratford. He received at least 20 commendations, including the Albert Gallatin Award at his retirement.

In 1969 the Coast Guard removed the fourth-order Fresnel lens and installed a rotating DCB-224 aerobeacon. To make room for the larger equipment they had to remove the lantern from the tower, leaving it "headless." The Coast Guard then donated the lantern to the Stratford Historical Society at the request of town historian Lewis Knapp. The lantern was put on display in Boothe Memorial Park with a fourth-order Fresnel lens inside. The lens came from Stratford Shoal Light and had been removed when that light was automated. The lens was later taken out of the park display because it was blinding drivers on Main Street.

The light at Stratford Point was eventually automated and the last Coast Guard crew left in May 1978. After a few years of vacancy, the Coast Guard decided to use the 1881 dwelling as housing for a Coast Guard family. In the late 1980s Senior Chief Paul Vanderkaay and his family were the residents.

The Coast Guard came to realize that the geographic range of the light could be improved by putting a lantern back on the tower along with a modern FA-251 optic. Vanderkaay knew that the lighthouse's original lantern was on display in the town. The Boothe Memorial Park Committee gave its blessing for the return of the lantern to the Coast Guard, and it was hoisted by crane into its rightful position atop the tower in late June 1990. On hand was a very happy Dan McCoart Jr.

The Coast Guard held an official rededication ceremony on July 14, 1990. Lewis Knapp addressed the crowd, saying, "Once in a great while, everything works out perfectly. This has been such an occasion, thanks to the vision and teamwork of many people. It demonstrates what we can achieve when we really care, and when we are not willing to settle for second best. Congratulations to the Coast Guard and the town!"

Captain Joseph J. Coccia, commanding officer of Coast Guard Group Long Island Sound, lived at the station with his family for a few years before leaving in 2004. There has been some limited public access in the past but the station is presently off limits, so currently you'll have to be content with the view past a wire fence at the end of Prospect Drive in Stratford. The light continues as an active aid to navigation with two white flashes every 20 seconds produced by a VRB-25 optic, at least the eighth generation of lighting apparatus in this lighthouse.

CHAPTER 12

Five Mile Point Light in October 2004. *Photo by the author.*

Five Mile Point Light

(New Haven Harbor Light)
1805, 1847

The three decades that this lighthouse served as an active aid to navigation pale in comparison to its long tenure as the centerpiece of a popular municipal park. It may have lost its navigational significance to offshore Southwest Ledge Light in 1877, but this graceful tower occupies a firm place in the hearts of the thousands who swim at the nearby beach or ride the carousel at Lighthouse Point Park each summer.

Established in 1638 based on its sheltered harbor at the confluence of three rivers and two creeks, New Haven was for many years one of New England's most prosperous cities. In 1810 the *American Gazetteer* reported, "As to pleasantness of situation and salubrity of air, New Haven is hardly exceeded by any city in America." The prominence of the "Elm City" was due in part to the presence of Yale College, which moved there from Saybrook in 1716.

Long before there was a lighthouse at Five Mile Point (so named because it is five miles from the center of New Haven) the spot was noted for a battle in the Revolutionary War when American riflemen repelled a British attempt to land and invade the city. The British later landed at Five Mile Point and set fire to the house of Amos Morris. Morris repaired his house and it still stands, not far from Lighthouse Point Park.

The first lighthouse at Five Mile Point was erected in 1805 during the period when the China trade and seal hunting from New Haven were flourishing. From 1801 to 1807 more than $1 million worth of goods passed through the port of New Haven each year, but the Embargo Act of 1807 cut the city's maritime trade by half.

Amos Morris died in 1801. The lighthouse was built on land sold to the federal government for $100 by his son, Amos Morris Jr., who served briefly as the first keeper. The 30-foot octagonal wooden tower was constructed by New London carpenter and stonemason Abisha Woodward, and its fixed white light was produced by eight lamps and 13-inch parabolic reflectors. A small one-and-a-half-story keeper's dwelling was built at the same time.

One of the early keepers, Greenwich native Jonathan Finch, spent 16 years (from 1805 to 1821) at Five Mile Point, apparently augmenting

Five Mile Point Lighthouse and keeper's house in 1996. *Photo by the author.*

his meager keeper's salary by taking in guests. It isn't known how long Finch engaged in this practice, which was generally frowned on by the authorities. An ad in the June 28, 1810, edition of the *American Mercury* read:

> *A SUMMER RETREAT. Gentlemen and Ladies, who, during the summer months, wish to enjoy a delightful sea breeze, an extensive prospect, shady bowers, &c. &c. are invited to the LIGHT-HOUSE, at the south point of New-Haven harbor, where arrangements are made for their accommodation. —Lobsters, fish, clams &c. taken directly from their natural element, and served up at a short notice, with the best trimmings —Liquors of the first chop —Pasture or stabling for horses. —Gentlemen who have passed their grand climactic, may here have their* mental *faculties perfectly restored in three days. —No cure, no pay. J. FINCH.*

Finch died in 1821 and was replaced by his son, William, who himself died three years later. The next keeper, Elihu Ives, remained for 22 years.

An 1832 publication by Robert Mills reported that the light was 50 feet above the sea. It served as a guide for both coastal and harbor traffic, according to Mills. He added that since some trees had been cleared, it could be seen better from the east.

In an 1838 report Lt. George M. Bache described the tower as "very much decayed" and leaky, and said that none of the lights were in the proper position. He also reported the keeper's house to be "in a very bad state of repair." The light was also deemed too low and dim to be much of a help to navigation. There was some consideration given to the idea of a new lighthouse offshore on Southwest Ledge, a more advantageous location. But building a lighthouse on the rocky ledge was then prohibitively expensive. Instead, $10,000 was appropriated for a new, taller tower at Five Mile Point on March 3, 1847.

The new 80-foot octagonal tower was constructed by contractor Marcus Bassett using brownstone from the East Haven quarry of Jabez Potter. The stone was brought to Five Mile Point by horse-drawn drays. The interior was lined with New Haven brick, and a circular granite stairway with 74 steps was added. A system of 12 lamps and reflectors was installed inside the cast-iron lantern, with the light 97 feet above sea level. A new two-and-one-half-story brick keeper's house was also erected.

An inspection in 1850, when Stephen Willard was keeper at $350 per year, reported:

> *This establishment is nearly new, all of which we must call in good order, although the tower leaks some, and one corner of the dwelling has settled. Lantern and lighting apparatus were clean; reflectors 22-inch, and first-rate. Put on a full set of iron burners; those that we left last year, which ought to last many years. Dwelling was, I am sorry to say, not so clean as the light-house.*

The multiple lamps and reflectors were replaced by a fourth-order Fresnel lens in 1855. The station's fog bell was run by a hot air engine in the 1860s, which was replaced in the 1870s by a Stevens striking apparatus that the keeper had to wind every few hours in times of fog.

Captain Elizur Thompson, born in East Haven in 1809, became keeper in 1860. As it turned out, he was the light's last keeper, staying until 1877 except for a two-year gap from 1867 to 1869. Thompson's wife, Elizabeth (Bradley), was an assistant keeper for two years, and their sons Sidney and George also served as assistants.

Charles William Bradley of East Haven was keeper during Elizur Thompson's two-year absence. His varied career included stints as a schoolteacher, farmer, postmaster, selectman, and justice of the peace.

When Southwest Ledge Light was established offshore in 1877, the old light at Five Mile Point was extinguished. Thompson went to Southwest Ledge to serve as the first keeper. After almost five years in that position, he returned to live in the old keeper's house at Five Mile Point, flying storm signal flags for the U.S. Weather Bureau. An 1890 article in the *New York Times* described the 81-year-old veteran keeper:

Capt. Elizur Thompson . . . still climbs the steps of the tower with agility to display the signals. He is a hospitable man and very popular among the professors of Yale College. . . . He is an authority on matters of local history that have transpired during the past seventy years.

Among many other interesting incidents, Thompson remembered shaking Gen. Lafayette's hand when the general was visiting the area in 1824, when Thompson was 15. Thompson's colorful life also included a journey to California during the gold rush of 1849.

When Elizur Thompson died in 1897, an obituary said, "There is hardly a mariner along the Sound who has not been guided by the light on the point at Morris Cove, and has not been thankful for its keeper, Capt. Thompson, for the reliance he could always place upon it."

In 1896 Five Mile Point Lighthouse was transferred to the War Department. For some years it was leased to a man named Albert Widmann, who made improvements to the site, including the addition of a boat landing. In 1922 the land was transferred to the state of Connecticut and the buildings to the city of New Haven, and in 1924 the city bought the entire property for $11,180.

The New Haven Park Commission opened Lighthouse Point Park with the city's only public swimming beach. Ball fields were added, and Babe Ruth, Ty Cobb, and Walter Johnson are said to have been among the major leaguers who visited for games. According to legend, Ruth once clubbed a ball that left the confines of the park and was stopped only by an electric power line.

Old Light, Light House Point, New Haven, Conn.

Postcard from the early 1900s. *From the author's collection.*

A carousel was established in a pavilion at Lighthouse Point in 1916, virtually in the shadow of the lighthouse. The beautiful wooden horses, plus one camel and two dragon chariots, fell to ruin after the carousel closed in 1976. A few years later the Friends of the Lighthouse Park Carousel restored the carousel to its former splendor. It reopened in 1985 and is now operating in season.

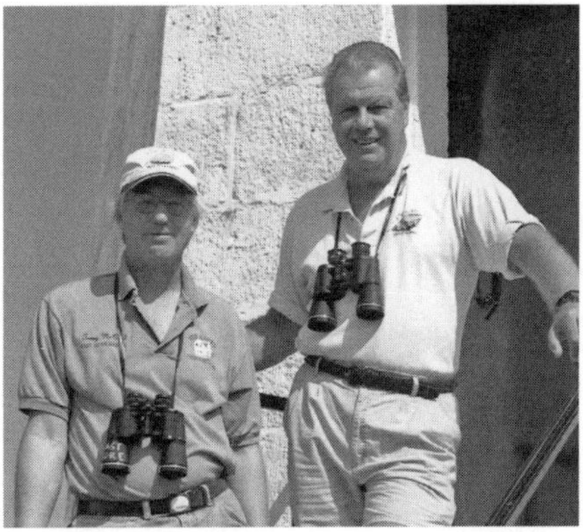

Lighthouse Point Park rangers Terry McCool and Phil Vallie in August 2003. *Photo by the author.*

In 1943 Lawrence Porter moved into the old keeper's house as manager of Lighthouse Point Park. Part of Porter's job was to hoist storm signal flags on a steel tower near the lighthouse. During his stay of more than 20 years, the hurricane of 1944 had the ocean lapping at his door, and another storm left five inches of water on the first floor of the house.

A $67,000 renovation of the lighthouse was completed in 1986. The interior and exterior of the tower were steam-cleaned, and guano accumulated over the decades was removed from the stairs. Plexiglas was installed in the lantern room, and chips in the mortar were repaired.

A city worker now uses the old keeper's house as his residence, but there has been recent discussion of turning the dwelling into a maritime museum. The grounds are open year-round, but the tower is usually closed. In October 2002 the Lighthouse Point Park rangers started offering tours of the lighthouse on a limited, reservations-only basis. Call (203) 946-8790 to see if any tours are scheduled.

There is a fee charged to visit Lighthouse Point Park in the summer. To get there from the north, take I-95 South to Exit 51. At the traffic light, take a left onto Townsend Avenue. Take a right onto Lighthouse Road and follow it to the park. From the south, take I-95 North to Exit 50 (Woodward Avenue). At the second traffic light, take a right onto Townsend Avenue, then take a right onto Lighthouse Road and follow it to the park.

CHAPTER 13

Southwest Ledge Light in 2002. *Photo by the author.*

Southwest Ledge Light

1877

Treacherous Southwest Ledge, about a mile offshore in the middle of the main shipping channel into New Haven Harbor, posed a major danger to local shipping traffic. By the 1870s the old lighthouse onshore at Five Mile Point was deemed inadequate, adding urgency to the call for a lighthouse on Southwest Ledge. "In approaching the harbor from the eastward the light is not visible until nearly abreast of it," wrote Maj. G. K. Warren of the Army Corps of Engineers, "being shut out by the woods. . . . If the light-house was on the ledge, vessels could run for it until it was close aboard, then haul to the northward, pass to the westward of the light, and head up the harbor. . . . The light-house would also serve as an excellent channel mark, by day as well as by night." Major Warren also pointed out that the woods around the old lighthouse deadened the fog bell so that it could be heard only a few hundred feet to the west.

In April 1872 I. C. Woodruff, engineer for the Third Lighthouse District, suggested a stone lighthouse similar to the one built in Fisher's Island Sound at Race Rock, at an estimated cost of $117,800. Instead the Lighthouse Board decided to erect a cast-iron superstructure doubling as living quarters atop a prefabricated cast-iron tubular foundation. This type of construction became standard for lighthouses built on submerged sites at offshore locations, but Southwest Ledge Lighthouse is one of the earliest examples.

On March 3, 1873, Congress appropriated $50,000 for the new lighthouse, and work began on the foundation. A layer of concrete about four feet thick was added to level the surface of the ledge. Two courses of masonry, each 18 inches thick, were added on top of the concrete, and the cast-iron foundation was rested on the masonry. The foundation consisted of cast-iron plates six feet high, four feet wide, and two inches thick, bolted together to form a tube 30 feet high and 24 feet in diameter. The tube was filled with concrete and surrounded by thousands of tons of granite riprap.

A severe winter storm struck during this stage of construction and damaged some of the work, but much progress was made during the working season of 1876. According to the Annual Report of the

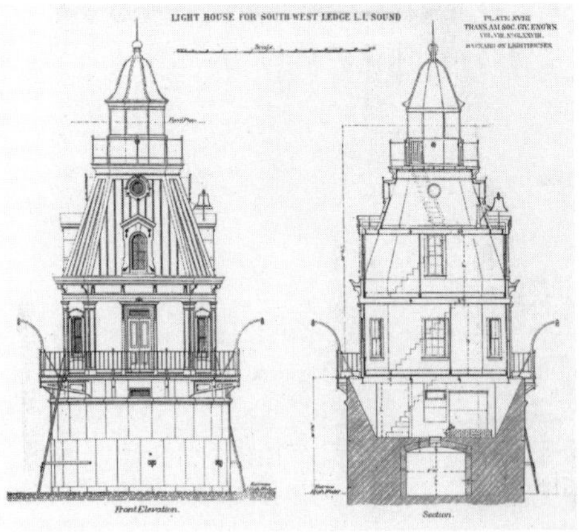

Plans for Southwest Ledge Light. *Courtesy of U.S. Coast Guard.*

Lighthouse Board, an additional section was added to the iron tube to increase its height and thus place the superstructure beyond risk of danger from high seas or ice.

The iron superstructure for Southwest Ledge was one of two identical ones built by the Baltimore firm of Ramsey and Carter. The other was created for Ship John Shoal Lighthouse in the Delaware Bay. The Connecticut site was ready first, so one superstructure went to New Haven while the other was displayed for a few months at the Centennial Exhibition of 1876 in Philadelphia, with an actual lighthouse keeper maintaining a light and a revolving fourth-order lens in the tower.

Southwest Ledge Lighthouse was finished in late 1876 and the light, 57 feet above sea level, was exhibited for the first time on January 1, 1877. The tower is 45 feet tall. The brick-lined basement originally held two water cisterns and was topped by a first floor, attic, watchroom, and lantern. The interior, other than the basement, was lined with beaded tongue-and-groove boards.

A few years after the light was established, a system of three detached granite breakwaters was constructed at the entrance to New Haven Harbor, largely because of the efforts of Capt. Charles H. Townshend. The east breakwater had its southwest terminus at the lighthouse site.

Other than its twin at Ship John Shoal, there's no lighthouse in the United States that resembles the one at Southwest Ledge. Its detailing is classified as Second Empire, with an octagonal lantern rising from a mansard roof. The overall effect is certainly handsome and striking. But living conditions were another story.

The 1879 report of the Lighthouse Board stated:

> *This station is much complained of by the keepers as taking in every rain, and being very damp and uninhabitable. The water*

which is caught from the roof into the tanks is also complained of as not being fit for drinking purposes. The landing spaces left in the riprap breakwater surrounding the light-house structure are again filled up with stones, which have been forced into them during the winter's storms. Efforts will be made to remedy both these evils during the year.

Some "slight repairs" were carried out by 1880, and the tower was painted red. Indeed, most cast-iron lighthouses in the United States were painted red or brown in the nineteenth century. Ship John Shoal Lighthouse is still painted a rusty shade of red.

The first keeper at Southwest Ledge was Elizur Thompson of East Haven, who had been the last keeper at the old lighthouse at Five Mile Point. An undated newspaper report in the collection of the Whitney Library of the New Haven Colony Historical Society describes the lighthouse when Thompson was in charge:

To be sure, the lighthouse keeper is married, and the feminine presence has expressed itself in refinements which enshrine the Lares and Penates of the custodians of that light in a comfortable home, and when the curtains are drawn it is cheerful there, even though the channel is choked with ice and a blizzard blows as if it would rock the iron walls off their foundation.

And besides keeping the glass house which contains the illuminating apparatus 54 feet over the sea level burnished, and the light, which, in clear weather, can be seen at night 12 miles away, the keeper must always keep an eye open for thick weather. He must rise twice during the hours of darkness and trim and rub the moisture off the panes of glass. . . .

No ferry or telegraph links them with the mainland, and no wharf is there to make a landing easy. The only way ashore is by a private boat which hangs far out from the little railing high up above the surface of the sea. . . .

Captain Thompson and his courageous wife have five rooms with household luxuries. Last summer a piano was taken across, and it was found, after the difficult landing had been made, that the instrument had shipped some water, but when pumped out and oiled, it was found to serve well enough to cheer up the evening after the lights had been lit within.

. . . The jolly lighthouse keeper . . . is the possessor of medals, which tell the tale of many brave deeds. He does not wear them on his breast like as a bicycle rider or a roller skater wears his trophies; they are stowed away in a drawer, and he does not care to talk about them.

Elizur's son, Henry C. Thompson, served as an assistant until his father left in 1881. Henry then became the head keeper, staying until 1896.

A second-class Daboll trumpet fog signal, powered by a hot-air engine, was put into operation in August 1888. The following year a red pane was added to the lantern to warn mariners of Branford Reef and Gangway Rock. An improved fog signal with a second-class trumpet operated by compressed air was established in March 1897.

Repairs may have improved the damp conditions somewhat, but life at an offshore lighthouse like this one was no picnic, particularly in winter. The isolation and harsh conditions may have contributed to the suicide of one assistant keeper, Nils Nilson, in January 1908. According to one man who had befriended Nilson, it was a preventable tragedy.

In June of 1904, while he was an assistant keeper at Sakonnet Lighthouse in Rhode Island, Nilson (sometimes reported as Nelson) had daringly rescued a drowning man whose boat had smashed on the rocks, and he received a Gold Life-saving Medal for his trouble. Three and a half years later Rev. J. O. Bergh of the Seamen's Bethel in New Haven observed that Nilson was exhibiting signs of mental illness. He tried to have the assistant keeper hospitalized or arrested, but was told that nothing could be done as long as Nilson hadn't committed a crime.

Nilson behaved erratically over a period of months. In late 1907 he threatened to kill the head keeper, Jorgen Tonneson. Nilson was described as a "strapping big fellow" and Tonneson rightly feared for his life. He brought his brother-in-law, Bernt Thorstensen, to live at the lighthouse for extra protection. Two or three times Thorstensen and Tonneson prevented Nilson from taking his own life with a butcher knife.

On January 21 Nilson went ashore and was seen asking for a knife at the Seaman's Bethel. He was subsequently found dead near a public dock. The medal-winning hero and once-reliable worker had cut his own throat. Keeper Tonneson had never notified the lighthouse authorities of the situation, and local officials had done nothing when Rev. Bergh had requested intervention.

By 1911 some of the joints in the cast-iron caisson had split apart, and it was strengthened with straps and buckles. During the Depression more riprap was added around the lighthouse, and a pair of boat cranes were built on concrete pads on the riprap to the north and south of the lighthouse.

Edward Grime, an assistant keeper, resigned in 1916. He cited the tower's dampness, poor water supply, and an abundance of cockroach-

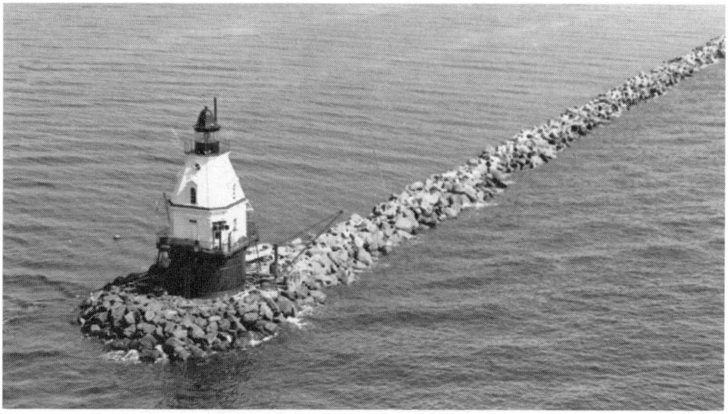

Southwest Ledge Light eventually became the southwest terminus of the east breakwater in New Haven Harbor. *U.S. Coast Guard photo.*

es. The living conditions must have been made somewhat more bearable in the ensuing decades, but unfortunately little information is available on the keepers during that period.

The Coast Guard, perhaps mercifully, destaffed Southwest Ledge Lighthouse in the summer of 1953. At that time the old kerosene-fueled IOV (incandescent oil vapor) lamp was replaced by new electrical equipment. The hand-cranked compressor and 1927 Tyfon foghorn were replaced by a new electric siren. The station's power came from a submarine cable with a switch onshore at Morgan Point (in East Haven, not to be confused with Morgan Point Lighthouse in Noank). The last Coast Guard crew of four men was reassigned, and a man called a lamplighter had the job of turning the light on and off from shore, as well as servicing the equipment as needed.

In the 1980s the Coast Guard considered removing the lighthouse superstructure and replacing it with a low-maintenance fiberglass tower on the original caisson. Luckily the structure has survived. After being boarded up and plagued by rampant rust, it's been nicely spruced up in recent years. In early 2001 the crew of the Coast Guard cutter *Penobscot Bay* out of Bayonne, New Jersey, conducted some maintenance work.

The Fresnel lens was replaced by an FA-251 optic in 1988, and later by the presently active VRB-25. The light, flashing red every five seconds, and foghorn continue to operate as official aids to navigation.

Southwest Ledge Light can be seen distantly from Lighthouse Point Park, but it is best seen by private boat.

CHAPTER 14

Early 1900s postcard of Sperry Light. *From the author's collection.*

3994

Sperry Light

(New Haven Light, New Haven Outer Breakwater Light)

1900; destroyed 1933

During a period of improvements to New Haven Harbor in the late nineteenth century, the Lighthouse Board decided that a lighthouse should be established on the eastern end of the outermost (west) of three granite breakwaters at the entrance to the harbor. The light would guide vessels into the harbor and also prevent them from colliding with the breakwater. The Lighthouse Board asked for $45,000 for this purpose in 1896, but only $25,000 was appropriated the following year. The board rethought the plans and announced that the new lighthouse would cost $75,000, and they received the additional $50,000 in a July 1, 1898, appropriation.

By April 1899 the cast-iron caisson for the lighthouse was completed, and in June it was lashed to a scow and towed to its position by the local tug *James H. Hogan.* The ocean bottom where the cylinder was to be placed was muddier than expected, so the area was dredged and covered with gravel. While the cylinder was being lowered, its watertight seal ruptured and it sank quickly to the bottom. When it landed, it "had a tilt like the Tower of Pisa," according to John Post's recollections in a 1948 letter to the *New Haven Register*. Post also recalled, "During the commotion a workman fell into the tub [caisson] and was drowned."

The tilt was corrected and eventually the cast-iron superstructure of the lighthouse was added atop the caisson. More than 13,000 tons of granite riprap was placed around the caisson for protection, and another 2,000 tons was added the following year. A fourth-order Fresnel lens showing a flashing red light, 61 feet above the water, was established along with a second-class fog siren operated by a 13-horsepower oil engine and compressed air. This fog signal was replaced by a "blower siren" with a two-horsepower oil engine in early 1903. The reason for the downgrade was that the vibrations caused by the earlier, more powerful siren were damaging to the lighthouse.

The lighthouse was at first referred to as New Haven Outer Breakwater Light, but it was soon nicknamed "Sperry Light" after local favorite son Rep. Nehemiah Day Sperry, who had been instrumental in bringing improvements to New Haven's harbor and shipping facilities. The official name was changed in 1912 to New Haven Light.

The first keeper was William DeLuce, who went on to become keeper at Connecticut's Green's Ledge Light. He was assigned an assistant, Bernard Francisco. Samuel Armour, who had been the final keeper at Sheffield Island Light in Norwalk, replaced DeLuce in 1902.

Although not that far from land, Sperry Light could be an isolated and lonely station in winter and times of heavy seas. According to a

Two local young men enjoy hockey practice near Sperry Light in 1934. The skeleton tower in the background had just been erected to replace the lighthouse. *Courtesy of Gunther Hall Publishing.*

1933 article in the *New Haven Register*, "Attaches of the Seamen's Bethel on Water Street [in New Haven] have made frequent trips to the lighthouse as well as to the boats in the outer harbor to bring cheer in the way of newspapers and magazines to the lonely mariners and keepers of the light."

Sperry Light had a chronic structural problem; the caisson cracked and had to be secured with iron straps. It was a losing battle, though, and in 1933 officials decided to remove the lighthouse and install an automated light on a steel skeleton tower.

Connecticut resident Ed Skvorc visited the site of the old lighthouse in September 2001 and made this report:

> *After almost 70 years of neglect the caisson foundation is like an old barrel with split sides. You can see the gaping cracks in the cast iron and the straps used to mend them. The cement that once filled the caisson is not much more than loose gravel and sand. There is some brickwork that was probably the cistern. There are rusty pipes and what must be reinforcing rods that were in the cement. It's ironic that the foundation that failed and doomed the lighthouse is the only thing that remains.*
>
> *I grew up looking at these breakwalls all my life and never even knew there was once a lighthouse there. I am saddened that this lighthouse could not have been saved, but I know after looking at the remains of the foundation that it was best to tear it down before the 1938 hurricane which would have almost certainly destroyed the lighthouse and probably have killed the poor keepers inside.*

An automated light on a skeleton tower remains in use here today, with a light that flashes white every four seconds.

CHAPTER 15

Faulkner's Island Light in September 2002. *Photo by the author.*

Faulkner's Island Light

1802

This venerable lighthouse has been called the Eiffel Tower of Long Island Sound. It's been rescued from the brink of oblivion in recent years by the valiant and vigilant volunteers of Faulkner's Light Brigade. Despite the tragic loss of the keeper's house to fire in 1976, this is one of Long Island Sound's brightest preservation sagas.

Little (less than three acres) crescent-shaped Faulkner's Island is about four miles from Guilford Harbor. The pleasant coastal town of Guilford traces its roots to 1639, when Rev. Henry Whitfield and a small band of Puritans settled in an area between the East River and Stony Creek, about midway between New Haven and Saybrook. The squaw Shaumpishuh, sachem of the Menunkatuck Indians, deeded the land to Whitfield's party in exchange for various trinkets.

Guilford Plantation, Connecticut's seventh settlement, was named for a town in Surrey, England, the former home of many of the early settlers. Whitfield's 1639 stone house, the oldest dwelling in the state, is open to the public as the Henry Whitfield State Museum.

Faulkner's Island had a number of owners in its pre-lighthouse days, when it was known as Falcon Island. Andrew Leete, son of a Connecticut governor, owned it for a time in the late 1600s. It became the property of brothers Caleb and Ebenezer Stone in 1715, and would remain in the Stone family for the rest of the century.

Guilford postmaster and tavern owner Medad Stone bought the island from his distant relative Noah Stone in 1800 for $158.34. The shrewd new owner apparently had an inkling that the government was formulating plans for a lighthouse on the island. In his comprehensive book *The Island Called Faulkner's*, historian Joel Helander tells of a 1791 boat trip taken by presidents-to-be Thomas Jefferson and James Madison. The sight of lonely Falcon Island in its prominent spot on the sound apparently made a strong impression on the men, who also spent some time at Medad Stone's tavern in Guilford.

As maritime traffic in the sound increased, wrecks on the reefs near the island became commonplace. There was also growing coastal trade out of Guilford, and it became apparent that a lighthouse was needed. On March 3, 1801, Congress appropriated $6,000 for that purpose. Faulkner's Island Light was the first lighthouse Thomas Jefferson authorized as president.

Helander suspects that there were open lines of communication between Medad Stone and government officials concerning lighthouse plans in 1800, prior to the purchase of the island from Noah Stone. In any case, Medad Stone sold the island to the government on May 12, 1801, for $325, more than twice what he had paid a year earlier. He initially had asked for $500.

The name "Falcon Island" seems to have originated with early settlers who may have mistaken osprey near the island for falcons. Around 1800 the common spelling of the name of the island changed from Falcon to Faulkner's. Faulkner was one of many variations used in England for the word "falconer," one who trains falcons for hunting and sport.

On official maps and charts the island's name has also been spelled "Falkner's" or "Falkner," stemming from an 1891 effort of the U.S. Board on Geographic Names to shorten place names and banish apostrophes. "Faulkner's" remains the preferred spelling with the local populace.

The man hired to construct the lighthouse was stonemason Abisha Woodward of New London, who had previously built the first lighthouse at Bald Head Island, North Carolina (1794), and the second New London Harbor Lighthouse (1801). Woodward completed the lighthouse on Faulkner's Island for $5,500. The octagonal 41-foot tower was constructed of brownstone blocks lined with "rough stone."

The original lighting system of twelve spider lamps (a shallow brass pan containing oil and several solid wicks) fueled by whale oil went into operation in the summer of 1802. The first keeper was Guilford sea captain Joseph Griffing at a salary of $200 per year. Not coincidentally, Griffing was the second cousin of the wife of Medad Stone.

One winter day in 1805, Keeper Griffing looked west and saw that a ship had gone aground on the rocks at nearby Goose Island. The keeper hurried to the scene in his small boat only to find all seven men aboard the wrecked vessel dead. The scene must have been heart wrenching, as the men had frozen to death as they huddled in a feeble attempt to stay warm. The identity of the ship and its crew was never determined. Griffing carefully buried the bodies in the shallow soil of Goose Island. Years later another keeper found the men's remains disinterred by the action of the sea. The keeper dug a new grave, protected by a barrier of stones.

A painfully small one-and-one-half-story wood-frame keeper's dwelling had been erected along with the lighthouse in 1802. In 1809 the ubiquitous Medad Stone went to bat for Keeper Griffing and complained to Secretary of the Treasury Albert Gallatin about the keeper's house, which Stone called a "shammy piece of business" with "no chambers fit for a dog to sleep in." During the following year an addition to the house was authorized and subsequently completed for a little over $300.

Griffing resigned in 1812, but enjoyed a long retirement and lived to the age of 86. He was replaced by Solomon Stone of Guilford, who moved to the island with his wife, Thankful, and their six children. It should come as no surprise that Solomon was the nephew of Medad Stone.

With the onset of the War of 1812, the next few years were tumultuous ones in Long Island Sound. British vessels lurked ominously off the shores of Guilford, and one day some soldiers from a warship landed a small craft at Faulkner's Island.

As the British landing craft approached, Keeper Stone hastily helped his three sons hide under some hay while his three daughters hid in compartments under the bake ovens. An officer entered the kitchen and approached the nervous Thankful Stone, who surely feared the worst. But the officer calmly and politely told her that the family had nothing to fear as long as they kept a good, clear light burning in the tower.

According to a 1934 article by Frederick Calvin Norton in the *Hartford Courant*, the British kept their word. The surgeon from a British ship was sent to the aid of Keeper Stone after he had sprained his ankle. Also according to Norton, Stone's "handsome" daughters were entertained as guests by the English officers. In fact, "no 'stones' were left unturned to make the occasion one long to be remembered in the lives of the participants."

But there were tense times before the end of the war, especially when the New London customs inspector ordered Stone to discontinue the light. Knowing that he could be putting himself and his family in danger, Stone complied. The British then threatened to blow up the lighthouse if it wasn't relighted, and Stone apparently requested and procured an order to reinstate the light. Disaster was narrowly averted thanks to Stone's levelheadedness.

Solomon Stone resigned his position in 1818, and the arrival of Eli Kimberly as keeper ended the Stone family's long association with the island. Another Guilford native, Kimberly had been a crewman on the revenue cutter *Eagle*. When he took the position at Faulkner's, Kimberly and his wife, Polly, had two small children and another on the way. Their third child was born only ten days after they arrived. Nine more children would be born to the Kimberlys during their long stay.

Kimberly's 33-year tenure saw gradual improvements on the island. The spider lamps in the lighthouse were replaced by a system of 12 oil lamps and parabolic reflectors. The deteriorating dwelling was repaired and enlarged in 1837, and the contractors also did some repointing and other repairs to the tower. A report by Lt. George M. Bache in 1838 gave a mixed review:

> *This light is serviceable to vessels passing through the sound, or seeking the anchorage to the northward of Falkner's island; its elevation is 93 feet, and its limit of visibility 15½ miles. . . . The tower, 40 feet in height, is of freestone, laid in courses, and ascended by an interior stairway of wood. The lantern is furnished with twelve lamps with reflectors, and eight lenses, which are placed around two circular tables, so as to display the light in every direction. . . .*
>
> *The lantern leaks and is badly ventilated; the circular ventilators at the bottom of its frame, and the cribbed holes above, have been entirely closed up.*

In 1840 a new, properly ventilated cast-iron lantern was installed, along with a system of nine lamps with 16-inch parabolic reflectors.

Offshore light stations like Faulkner's Island were lonely and isolated in winter, but they often buzzed with visitors in summer. According to historian Joel Helander it was not unusual for the keepers to welcome a hundred people on a summer's day at Faulkner's. The Kimberlys were known as excellent hosts, and the keeper even built a bowling alley with a well-stocked bar.

Sadly, their hospitality backfired on the Fourth of July in 1829, when a pack of 20 young men from New Haven drank themselves senseless and proceeded to tear apart the Kimberlys' vegetable garden. It went from bad to worse as the small mob smashed some lighting equipment in the lighthouse and destroyed the keeper's boat. A jury failed to find the young men guilty, but this incident apparently sparked the prohibition of liquor sales at American light stations.

Despite the efforts of the much-respected Keeper Kimberly, wrecks still occurred frequently around the island, and the keeper was involved in a number of rescues. It was reported in the 1840s that four vessels a year went aground on a reef east of the island. Late in Kimberly's tenure, buoys were belatedly placed to improve the situation.

Polly Kimberly died in 1845. Three years later Eli Kimberly remarried, and in 1851 he retired to life onshore. His replacement, Capt. Oliver N. Brooks, would become one of America's most revered keepers of the nineteenth century.

A native of Westbrook, Connecticut, Brooks had first gone to sea

Music was ever-present during the years Oliver Brooks was keeper. Here the keeper performs with his grandson, Oliver Brooks Husted, and Old Tige the singing Newfoundland dog. *From* The Island Called Faulkner's, *courtesy of Joel Helander.*

as a cabin boy at the age of 13 and had become captain of a vessel at 21. He and his wife, Mary, had their first child in 1849, and when Capt. Brooks learned of the pending retirement of Eli Kimberly he decided it was time to "settle down" to the relatively stable life of a light keeper.

Brooks's first few years on the island were eventful. In 1856 a new fourth-order Fresnel lens replaced the multiple lamps and reflectors, and in 1858 a new dwelling replaced the earlier one, which was described in the annual reports of the Lighthouse Board as dilapidated and unworthy of repair.

A daring rescue on November 23, 1858, by Keeper Brooks gained him widespread fame. A newspaper described the events:

> *The recent, courageous and even desperate act of Capt. Brooks, keeper of the Faulkner's Island Light, in rescuing the captain, his wife and crew, from a wreck in Long Island Sound, deserves more than a passing notice. . . . The wreck lay upon Goose Island, some two miles from this; but Capt. Brooks could see, with his glass, the persons in the rigging, and the sea lashed into unusual fury, making a breech high over its decks, and threatening instant destruction. It was too sad a sight for the brave man to endure, and provided as he was by the government with nothing but a small sailboat . . . he would have been fully justified in leaving them to a fate horrible to think of. His wife was on shore, and he was alone with his family of little children; but telling them of the peril he was about to assume . . . from which he might never return, he kissed them, and calling upon God to protect them and bless his endeavor, he jumped into the frail skiff and steered boldly into the storm and billows.*

The five people on the wrecked schooner, the *Moses F. Webb* from New Brunswick, saw Brooks approaching but felt their situation was hopeless. The newspaper account continued:

By the most skillful management of his boat, now shooting past, and once over the very wreck itself, he at last managed to pick them off, one at a time, and then turned for the shore. But it was only by constant bailing and tremendous efforts that the boat was kept above water, and at last reached the island, with its inmates exhausted, and nearly dead with hunger and exposure.

Brooks's two small daughters, Mary Ellen and Nannie (Nancy Amelia), greeted him with "tears and screams of joy," and the weary survivors were taken to the dwelling to rest. Sadly, about a half hour before the keeper arrived on the scene, the three-year-old daughter of the vessel's captain slipped from his grasp and was lost. But the others clearly owed their lives to the courageous keeper. The rescue was cited by many as one of the most daring and miraculous in memory, and for his trouble Brooks received a gold medal from the New York Life Saving Benevolent Association. He also got a raise in pay from $350 yearly to $500, thanks to the efforts of an admiring congressman.

Joel Helander's book *The Island Called Faulkner's* and newspaper articles of the era provide us with many more details of the Brookses' years on the island. Like the Kimberlys, the Brookses were warm hosts to government officials and tourists alike. One frequent guest was Professor Joseph Henry, the first chairman of the Lighthouse Board that was created in 1852 and also the first secretary of the Smithsonian Institution. Henry and Brooks became close friends.

Keeper Brooks was an avid hunter and an expert taxidermist. Over the years, the parlor of the keeper's dwelling came to be filled with dozens of beautifully displayed stuffed birds. Many of the birds died in collisions with the lighthouse lantern, not an uncommon occurrence at many light stations. During spring and fall migrations, hundreds of birds were sometimes killed in a night.

Brooks's older daughter, Mary Ellen, amassed a collection of beautiful aquatic plants. Her books of preserved specimens sometimes fetched $100 or more from collectors. Mary Ellen was also an accomplished watercolor artist. Like her father, she was a daring boat handler and a strong swimmer, and she sometimes assisted her father in rescues. In addition to all this, she was a fine musician and part of a small family "orchestra."

Captain Brooks sometimes played his flute or fife solo, but when the family gathered for musical sessions, he played the double bass. Mary Ellen played cello or violin, and Nannie played the piano. The ensemble was completed by an unlikely singer—a large Newfoundland dog named Old Tige. The dog's vocalizations were described by one visiting writer as "not the long howls of canine distress; nor yet were they ordinary barks, but a wonderful something in between."

Once when the automatic fog bell machinery failed and required replacement parts, Brooks rigged a rope from the bell to the house so that Mary and their daughters could ring it while he went to pick up the needed parts. As it turned out, fog necessitated the manual ringing of the bell for 48 hours during the keeper's absence. In 1879 a powerful, new first-class steam-driven fog whistle replaced the bell. The cistern and boilers for the signal were housed in an odd-looking A-frame wooden shed.

The year 1871 was one of many changes. A new 16-sided cast-iron lantern was installed, the tower was lined with brick, and the old wooden stairs were replaced by a circular iron stairway. A distinctive detail was added at this time—a short curved staircase leading from a door in the watchroom up to the lantern room gallery. The house was also enlarged to accommodate an assistant keeper, giving it the appearance it would retain for over a century.

Mary Brooks was appointed second assistant keeper in 1879. The position was abolished when the Brooks family left in 1882.

After retiring as keeper, Oliver Brooks moved briefly to California before returning to Guilford and serving in the state legislature. He died in 1913 at the age of 90. Subsequent keepers sometimes stayed for several years at Faulkner's, but none had the memorable impact of keepers Kimberly and Brooks. Between 1901 and 1934, 10 keepers and 40 assistants came and went.

In a February 2003 article in *Lighthouse Digest* magazine, Vivian Jensen Chapin wrote about her father Arthur Jensen's stint as Faulkner's Island keeper from 1911 to 1916. Jensen and his wife, Ingeborg, listened to recordings of Enrico Caruso on a Victrola for entertainment. When work and weather permitted, the Jensens would sometimes cruise up the Connecticut River to Essex or over to New London for Harvard–Yale races.

This photo of Faulkner's Island Lighthouse, the keeper's dwelling, and fog bell tower was taken in 1914 by Ingeborg Jensen, wife of Keeper Arthur Jensen. *Courtesy of Vivian Jensen Chapin.*

Vivian Jensen Chapin remembers her mother saying that she was never bored or lonesome on Faulkner's Island. She had a vegetable garden and a yard full of chickens, and also worked hard to keep the keeper's quarters spotless so it would pass muster during the lighthouse inspector's visits. An article on January 23, 1914, in the *Shoreline Times* told of the heroism of Ingeborg Jensen on an occasion when her husband was ill and the assistant keeper was ashore:

> *There arose a dense fog requiring the starting of the oil engine, which runs the fog siren. Few women, even had they the skill, could have mustered the strength to perform this feat, which is a task for a strong man. Yet Mrs. Jensen, knowing that the siren must be started and that there was no one but herself to do it, took hold of the fly wheel, five feet in diameter, rolled it back against the compression, and so started into action the machinery which sounded the warning siren. Mrs. Jensen ran the engine four hours, until the fog cleared away, and also lighted the lamp in the tower and watched it all night long. . . . Mrs. Jensen kept the station running that night, single handed, by sheer force of ability, and is entitled to much commendation.*

In February 1923 Assistant Keeper A. B. Brussiere, a native of Newark, New Jersey, left Guilford to return to Faulkner's Island with supplies. His boat was caught in drifting ice, and the engine became overheated and died. Brussiere rigged a makeshift sail and managed to navigate safely to Hammonasset Point in Madison, a few miles east of Guilford, after a five-hour battle.

Florida brothers Leonard and Sam Fuller served as keepers during Prohibition, and according to Joel Helander they received certain benefits in exchange for their hospitality to local rumrunners. Sam Fuller and an assistant were also involved in a dispute with local lobstermen that ended up costing them their lobstering license.

In October 1924 Keeper Sam Fuller narrowly escaped death when his slicker caught in the flywheel of his boat's engine and pulled him to the floor. The keeper was unconscious when Assistant Keeper Fred Braffire spotted the drifting boat and rushed to Fuller's aid. Fuller had five breaks in his right arm but recovered to have a long light-keeping career that extended well into the 1950s.

George Zuius was the last keeper for the civilian Lighthouse Service, leaving Faulkner's Island in 1941, when the Coast Guard took over. Zuius's daughter, Barbara, later remembered playing on the island with a pet chicken and her dog, Rexie. Keeper Zuius was on Faulkner's Island when the great hurricane of 1938 struck. He managed to keep the light going throughout the storm, but the boathouse was destroyed.

During the war years, a large contingent of Coast Guardsmen was present on the island, armed with rifles in case German U-boats made an appearance (they never did). Later there were typically four men assigned to the island, with three on duty at one time. The men had three weeks on the island followed by a one-week shore leave.

A 1965 article in the *New Haven Register* described island life under the Coast Guard. Harvey Holman, boatswain mate second class and the officer in charge, shared his feelings with the writer, Ted Eastwood. "No, I'm never lonely," he said, "and I never wish I was somewhere else. This is good duty. Being out here alone forces you to do things for yourself, to improvise." Dick Webb, another member of the crew, said winter could be tough. On the plus side, Webb enjoyed reading and going to the top of the lighthouse to think.

The most negative view came from Californian Robert Ewing. When asked how he liked winter on the island, Ewing replied, "The things I like best in this world are warm sunshine, fast cars, and women. Does that answer your question?"

By the 1970s the Coast Guard was formulating plans for the automation and destaffing of the station. But as it turned out, the era of Faulkner's Island as a staffed station came to an abrupt and depressing end on March 15, 1976.

A Coast Guard press release the next day stated dryly:

> *Fire destroyed the light tower and dwelling at this Coast Guard Light Station yesterday. A Coast Guard Group Long Island Sound rescue and assistance team assisted in fighting the fire and Coast Guard utility boats from Station New Haven and Aids to Navigation Team New Haven responded. All personnel were evacuated by the utility boats when the fire threatened the main fuel tank. A helicopter from Coast Guard Air Station Brooklyn later reported the fire out with the exception of minor brush fires. The rescue and assistance party overhauled the fire and reported there were no injuries associated with the incident.*

Fortunately, the rumors of the lighthouse tower's demise were greatly exaggerated—it was slightly scorched but unbowed. But the keeper's house was truly a thing of the past.

On the day of the fire, two of the four men assigned to the station, Mark Robinson and John Von Ogden, were away on leave. Robinson, the officer in charge, had left instructions for removing some paint from the molding around the portico roof outside the front door. A young seaman's apprentice used a disk grinder and a propane torch for the task, and by the time he realized a fire had started, it was too late to control it. After a fire pump malfunctioned, he and the other crewman on duty tried to fight the fire with handheld extinguishers, but their efforts were futile. Two Coast Guard cutters arrived, as did eight members of the Guilford Volunteer Fire Department, but the building was a total loss.

The official report on the incident stated that the fire was most likely electrical, caused by the disk grinder overloading a circuit. According to the report, there was no misconduct or negligence on anyone's part. Despite this finding, those in the know believed the true culprit was the propane torch. In any event, the fire was clearly an accident, but there were some sighs of relief from the Coast Guard, since automation could now proceed without any worry about the abandonment of the house.

With the demise of the dwelling and the automation of the light, nature began to reclaim Faulkner's Island. The island developed into one of the most important nesting sites for the endangered Roseate Tern, largely through the efforts of research wildlife biologist Dr. Jeffrey Spendelow. Spendelow and Fred Sibley started the Falkner Island Tern Project (FITP) in 1978. In 2002 the island was the site of the sixth-largest Roseate Tern colony (about 250 to 300 pairs) in the United States, but the numbers have declined since then. FITP staff and volunteers, using the light station's old engine house as a base, also have studied other nesting and migratory birds on the island and nearby Goose Island.

The island was incorporated into the new Connecticut Coastal National Wildlife Refuge, redesignated the Stewart B. McKinney National Wildlife Refuge in 1987. (McKinney was a congressman who had fought for the establishment of the refuge.) The island was handed over to the U.S. Fish and Wildlife Service, with the exception of the lighthouse itself.

The island has also had a large rabbit population, reportedly the descendants of a pair of tame rabbits left by a Coast Guard keeper in the 1970s. With no predators on the island, some of the rabbits died from starvation and parasites, while others froze to death in winter. In October 1980 a Humane Society "rescue team" removed 115 rabbits from the island. Those in good condition were put up for adoption. This effort failed to rid the island of rabbits, so it was repeated in the late 1990s. Nevertheless, the colony lives on, resistant to the attempts of nature and humans to end the rabbits' island stay.

In the late 1960s Coast Guard Keeper Steve Martin gave a tour of the station to a Guilford high school student named Joel Helander. In

1980, during a camping visit, Helander realized that the island was to him a true "island utopia." His research into Faulkner's past accelerated, culminating in his 1988 book, *The Island Called Faulkner's.* This book remains the ultimate source on this outpost on the sound.

Helander coordinated an open house on the island in August 1989, and it became a popular annual event. In January 1991 Helander was part of a 10-member group, "Friends of Faulkner's," who met at the Guilford Free Library and began to discuss ways to save the island and its lighthouse. In addition to an erosion problem, the tower had begun to fall into disrepair after automation. This preservation effort grew into the Faulkner's Light Brigade, a commission of the Guilford Preservation Alliance.

The town of Guilford became the administrator of the lighthouse restoration in partnership with Faulkner's Light Brigade, and a five-year license was procured from the Coast Guard to allow this partnership to assist with lighthouse maintenance. A partnership was also formed with the U.S. Fish and Wildlife Service. The town applied successfully through the Connecticut Department of Transportation for $250,000 in Intermodel Surface Transportation Efficiency Act (ISTEA) funding to restore the lighthouse. Another $50,000 raised by Faulkner's Light Brigade was added to the restoration funds.

In 1997 a Lighthouse Restoration Committee selected architect Walter Sedovic to prepare design plans, and later that year named International Chimney to perform the restoration work. Sedovic and International Chimney had previously worked together on the move of Block Island Southeast Lighthouse in Rhode Island.

Restoration was completed in late 1999. The work included a new ventilation system, the application of an all-white breathable coating to make the tower weathertight, painting the lantern gallery inside and out, a new lightning protection system, installation of a stainless steel door, new 12-pane casement windows in the face of the west wall, restoration of the original weathervane, and the scraping and painting of the interior handrail. Another major addition was a 75-square-foot entry deck made of Pau Lope, a dense tropical hardwood resistant to insects and decay. This restoration was an enormous stride forward, but a spring 2004 inspection showed a need for better ventilation and repainting of the stairway.

Keepers and others were long aware that Faulkner's Island was gradually being washed away by erosion, but little was done about it before the addition of a granite breakwater on the island's west side in the 1930s. The breakwater protected the boat-landing area but did nothing to halt the wearing away of the island, especially on the east side. Coast Guard keepers Mark Robinson and John Von Ogden recalled a storm when about two feet of the bluff fell away at one time.

Vital survey work by George T. Gdovin, affiliated with Little Harbor Laboratory of Guilford, confirmed the urgent erosion problem. Gdovin's geomorphic study of the island in transition became the subject of his master's thesis at Antioch University. With this scientific backing, Faulkner's Light Brigade soon got the erosion-control ball rolling.

With help from the Connecticut Trust for Historic Preservation and the National Trust for Historic Preservation, in September 1996 federal funds were appropriated for erosion control. The balance of the $4.5 million needed was appropriated in 1998 with the help of Senators Joseph Lieberman and Christopher Dodd as well as Rep. Rosa DeLauro.

By 2000 the lighthouse stood a mere 34 feet from the brink. In September of that year Zenone of Franklin, Massachusetts, brought an armada of heavy construction equipment to the island and began work under the direction of the Army Corps of Engineers. Work could not take place during the nesting season of the Roseate Tern, which runs from May through August.

William Parker, left, was stationed at Faulkner's Island Light Station as a Coast Guardsman in 1945–46. Joel Helander, right, was a catalyst in the formation of Faulkner's Light Brigade and wrote the definitive history of the island. *September 2002 photo by the author.*

In mid-December a southwesterly storm ripped into Zenone's landing barges. Icy gale-force winds of over 60 miles per hour combined with seven-foot waves to throw both barges onto the island's shore, and one of the barges was severely damaged. Despite the setbacks, Phase 1 of the erosion control work was finished in early 2001, providing protection from the island's north tip to a point 250 feet south of the lighthouse.

A massive stone wall nearly 20 feet high and 50 feet wide was installed along the east embankment, with an outer layer consisting of stones weighing as much as three tons each. Hardy vegetation was planted on the embankment to help buffer wind and rain. Next to the lighthouse for 300 feet, additional stability was created by the placement of six-inch-high "geo cells," a system of plastic fabric with holes, covered with earth and planted with vegetation. A length of 600 feet of the east embankment was stabilized under Phase 1 of the erosion control project. Phase 2 will include the construction of another 600-foot revetment "wrapping" the south end of the island.

A 200th birthday celebration for the lighthouse took place on the weekend of September 7 and 8, 2002. During the two-day open house, a total of 925 people toured the inside of the tower, guided by members of the Coast Guard's Aids to Navigation Team from New Haven.

Fred Farnsworth, chair of Faulkner's Light Brigade, spoke at a Saturday evening celebration at Jacobs Beach in Guilford. "This is more than a commemoration of Faulkner's Light," he said. "This is also a celebration of a successful campaign of preservation. . . . The campaign still isn't over. It was a long slog for eleven years!"

Joel Helander delivered an eloquent keynote address. "Night and day, in calm or tempestuous seas, in warm sunshine, swirling blizzards, or howling nor'easters," he said, "Faulkner's Light has created a sanctuary of security and trust. It is a monument to the American nautical soul." Helander concluded, "The grand dame of Long Island Sound is still the mariner's salvation. She is the story of survival and continuity. She remains preserved as a beacon of joy and security, an American symbol of hope and reliability." Helander dedicated the event to the ex-keepers who were present, and six of them took the stage to thunderous applause.

Darkness descended and the fireworks commenced. A huge air-powered foghorn removed many years ago from Faulkner's Island was sounded over and over again from a truck in the parking lot. The rich, satisfying sound was a fitting note on which to close.

You can see the lighthouse in the distance from Guilford's town marina. For more information about visiting during the annual open houses, contact Faulkner's Light Brigade, P.O. Box 199, Guilford, CT 06437. Visit their Web site at www.lighthouse.cc/FLB/. You may also phone them at (203) 453-8400.

CHAPTER 16

Lynde Point Light, October 2004. *Photo by the author.*

Lynde Point Light

(Saybrook Inner Light)
1803, 1838

Old Saybrook, on the west side of the entrance to the Connecticut River, was first settled in 1635 and incorporated as a town in 1852. The mighty Connecticut is New England's largest river, flowing from the Connecticut Lakes in northern New Hampshire to its mouth between Old Saybrook and Old Lyme. The growth of commerce along the river—navigable as far north as Hartford—as well as fishing based in Old Saybrook, led to increased shipping traffic.

To mark the river entrance and the harbor at Old Saybrook, the federal government resolved in 1802 to erect a lighthouse. Land was purchased from William Lynde for $225, along with a right-of-way through Lynde's farm.

An octagonal, shingled, wooden tower 35 feet tall and 20 feet in diameter at its base (and 8 feet in diameter at the top) was built for $2,200 by New London carpenter Abisha Woodward in 1803. An iron lantern 7 feet 3 inches high and 6 feet 10 inches in diameter was installed with a system of whale oil–fueled lamps and reflectors. The light went into service on August 17, 1803. An earlier dwelling already on the property served initially as the keeper's house.

The first lighthouse was criticized for being too dim and too short. An 1832 publication, *The American Pharos, or Light-House Guide* by Robert Mills, also pointed out an unusual problem. "This light house . . . stands on a low sandy point projecting into the sea, having on its west side a considerable tract of salt marsh, containing a pond of brackish water, which by its evaporation creates a mist, that at times very much impedes the light, the weather at the same time being clear off shore."

Some of the marshy flats around Lynde Point were filled in during the 1830s, but the area recently has been the subject of a salt marsh restoration project.

Lieutenant George M. Bache included Lynde Point in his important 1838 survey. He reported that the system of seven lamps with 8½-inch reflectors was not in proper alignment, and that an oil storage building was subject to flooding. The six-room dwelling was in good condition, but the wooden tower was "much decayed."

Some consideration was given to the possibility of making the wooden tower taller, but the Light-House Establishment authorities concluded that the most practical option was to build a new lighthouse. Two appropriations of $5,000 and $2,500 were passed in 1837 and 1838, and in August 1838 the contract was awarded to Jonathan Scranton, Volney Pierce, and John Wilcox. John Bishop of New London supervised the tower's construction. The new octagonal brownstone tower was 65 feet tall, 25 feet in diameter at the base and 12 feet at the top, and had walls 5 feet thick at the bottom and 2 feet thick at the top. An octagonal, wrought-iron lantern with a copper dome topped the structure.

An 1850 inspection noted that 10 lamps and reflectors were in use. Catherine (Sykes) Whittlesey was keeper at the time, having replaced her husband, Daniel, who died in 1841. The report read:

> *Light-house is a good building and in good order. Dwelling is a frame building; the sills and lower part of the house are decayed in consequence of the land being raised about two feet above the sills; this house ought to have been raised when the house was raised. There have been some conveniences added to the house since I supplied it—such as blinds to the windows. Lighting apparatus is good and in first-rate clean order, and so is everything in and about the premises.*

A fog bell was first established at Lynde Point in 1854, and various bells and striking machinery were used over the years. In 1858 a fourth-

Unlike most similar lighthouses, which have iron or stone stairways, Lynde Point Lighthouse has a wooden stairway. *Photo by the author.*

order Fresnel lens manufactured in France by Barbière and Fenestre replaced the multiple lamps and reflectors. That lens was in turn replaced in 1890 by a fifth-order lens that remains in use today. A new Gothic Revival keeper's house replaced the earlier dwelling in 1858.

Around 1868 a brick lining for the lighthouse was funded but never actually installed. A new wooden stairway was added at that time, and it survives in good condition. Around the same time the lantern was repaired. The 1869 Annual Report of the Lighthouse Board added, "The sea-wall which protects the site was damaged by the gales of last winter and is now being repaired."

One of the most interesting personalities in the history of this light station is John Ninde Buckridge. Born in New York City in 1833, Buckridge joined the U.S. Navy in 1851 and in the following year traveled on a store ship to the China Sea and Japan. The vessel was the first to leave China for Japan, where the Treaty of Friendliness was signed in 1854, and it was said that Buckridge was one of the first three Americans to sleep on Japanese soil following the signing of the treaty. He later sailed on the frigate *St. Lawrence* from Norfolk, Virginia, under Lt. Cdr. Joseph B. Hull.

Buckridge left the navy in 1859 but enlisted in the New York Heavy Artillery in 1862. While on a woodcutting detail at Brandy Station near Rappahannock, Virginia, his right leg was injured. His leg was soon amputated, which ended Buckridge's military career. After running a store for a few years in West Farms, New York, he joined the Lighthouse Service in 1877. Following six years as an assistant at Stepping Stones, Stratford Shoal, and Eaton's Neck lighthouses, he was assigned as keeper at Lynde Point on June 26, 1883.

John Ninde Buckridge was a well-loved and respected keeper and citizen during his 19 years at Lynde Point. According to an 1890 newspaper report, "The grounds about the light he has arranged in a strikingly beautiful manner, and in summer they blossom as a rose, and are a favorite resort." He and his wife, Margaret (Abel), had six children. Their son Thomas went on to become a lighthouse keeper at Saybrook Breakwater Light, among other locations.

The Buckridges' daughter Minnie married Ezra Kelsey of Westbrook, Connecticut, at the lighthouse on March 22, 1890. Although the day was described as bleak and blustery, nearly 100 people attended. The happy couple left "amid the hoarse screech of congratulatory steamer whistles on the river and the customary shower of rice and old slippers." Ezra Kelsey later became a lighthouse keeper at Rockland Lake Light on the Hudson River and Crown Point Light on Lake Champlain.

Margaret Buckridge narrowly escaped death or serious injury one day in April 1901 when a sudden gust of wind knocked her off the seawall near the lighthouse. She fell about ten feet to the rocks, fracturing several ribs and getting knocked unconscious in the process. When she came to, Margaret realized that the tide was coming in and that nobody could hear her cries for help. She managed to drag herself to safety and eventually recovered.

Keeper Buckridge's son Tom served as an unpaid assistant until his own marriage in 1901. John Ninde Buckridge retired from the Lighthouse Service the following year. When he died a decade later a newspaper obituary remembered him in fond terms: "Always good natured and possessing a keen sense of humor, he had a bright word or a joke for everyone with whom he came in contact up to within a few days of the end. He was one of nature's noblemen—'a gentleman of the old school.'"

Elmer Gildersleeve, a native of Port Jefferson, New York, succeeded Buckridge and remained keeper until 1925. His son Lawrence, born at the lighthouse in 1906, was interviewed in 1975 for an article in the *New Haven Register*. Lawrence, one of eight children born to Keeper Gildersleeve and his wife during the 34 years they spent at lighthouses in New York and Connecticut, said that he didn't remember ever being lonely as a child. To pass the time the family played cards, listened to the phonograph, or simply watched the parade of passing ships, from steamers to square-riggers. Young Lawrence made friends with the families who summered in the surrounding borough of Fenwick, and he earned a little extra cash by caddying at the nearby golf course. The pay was five cents for 18 holes, but Lawrence recalled, "If I was lucky I got a quarter tip."

Sometimes young Lawrence was sent out the front door to fish for the family's supper, and usually within about 20 minutes he'd catch some eels or flounder. To get to school, Lawrence had to walk across an old wooden plank bridge at South Cove to a building four and a half miles away. He also remembered helping railroaders turn their engines around on a turntable near Saybrook Point. For his trouble he'd get a free ride in the engine.

Lawrence went on to serve as a seaman, assistant cook, and later machinist on the lightship *Cornfield*, a little more than three miles offshore from Lynde Point Lighthouse. He was on the lightship during the hurricane of September 21, 1938, and recalled 20-foot seas pouring over the bow and down the smokestack. Another time ice floes moved the lightship five miles off its position, until it could be towed into New London.

A postcard of Lynde Point Light from the early 1900s. *From the author's collection.*

The hurricane of 1938 caused extensive cracks in the tower.

The 1858 keeper's house was razed and replaced by a modern duplex in 1966 despite some local objections. The light was converted to electricity in the 1950s and was automated in 1978. Among the last Coast Guard keepers was Boatswain Mate First Class Robert Horoschak. An Associated Press article about his wife, Violet, made it vividly clear that lighthouse life is not for everyone. "It's so boring, there's nothing to do," she complained. "It's a place to get fat, eat, lie around and watch TV. Even my dog's gained weight."

The station still serves as housing for two Coast Guard families. One of the residents in 2005 is Michael Allen, chief engineer for U.S. Coast Guard Aids to Navigation Team Long Island Sound, based in New Haven. The unit maintains about 1,500 aids from Greenwich to Watch Hill, Rhode Island, covering 240 miles of coastline on Long Island Sound, the Connecticut River, and other waterways. Although the equipment in the lighthouse normally runs just fine by itself, Allen likes to check things out much like a traditional keeper. He enjoys climbing to the lantern room to relax and says the sunsets are "amazing."

The road to the lighthouse is not open to the public. The tower can be seen from several spots along the shore, but the best views are from the occasional lighthouse cruises leaving Captain John's Sport Fishing Center in Waterford, Connecticut. Call (860) 443-7259 or visit www.sunbeamfleet.com for details. Camelot Cruises in Haddam, Connecticut, offers cruises that pass near the lighthouse; see www.camelotcruises.com or call (800) 522-7463.

CHAPTER 17

Saybrook Breakwater Light from the top of Lynde Point Light, October 2004. ***Photo by the author.***

Saybrook Breakwater Light

(Saybrook Outer Light)
1886

Today the picturesque town of Old Saybrook is the commercial center of the Lower Connecticut River Valley, but it was hindered in its early maritime development by a dangerous bar at the Connecticut River's mouth. Lynde Point Lighthouse was established in 1803 just inside the west side of the entrance to the river, and a buoy was placed to mark the bar in 1831. These aids proved insufficient for the increased maritime traffic, however.

Two granite breakwaters were built from opposite sides of the river mouth to delineate the newly dredged channel in the 1870s. Congress appropriated $20,000 for a lighthouse at the end of the west breakwater, about a mile and a half from Lynde Point Light, on August 7, 1882. The Lighthouse Board responded by saying the project could not be completed for less than $38,000.

It took two years but on July 7, 1884, the additional money was appropriated. In the meantime a temporary stake light had been placed at the end of the breakwater. During 1885 a subfoundation was completed on the river bottom. Then a cylindrical cast-iron caisson, 32 feet high and 30 feet in diameter, was sunk into position in about 17 feet of water. The caisson was filled with concrete, with a space left to serve as the lighthouse basement and cistern.

The cast-iron components of the 49-foot lighthouse tower were fabricated by the G. W. and F. Smith Iron Company in Boston. The superstructure was assembled and then lined with brick. The overall design was similar to Connecticut's Stamford Harbor Lighthouse, built in 1882. Four levels below the 12-sided lantern and watchroom served as the keeper's living quarters, along with space for storage. The lower deck gallery roof and its supporting posts have recently been removed.

The lighthouse was completed and a fifth-order Fresnel lens exhibited a fixed white light for the first time on June 15, 1886, with its focal plane 58 feet above mean high water. A red sector was added in May 1889 to warn mariners of dangerous areas known as Crane Reef and the Hen and Chickens. On January 1, 1890, a fourth-order lens replaced the original one.

Early view of Saybrook Breakwater Light. *U.S. Coast Guard photo.*

A 1,000-pound fog bell with automatic striking machinery was added in 1889, replacing the fog signal at Lynde Point. A new Gamewell striking apparatus for the bell was installed a few years later. According to Harlan Hamilton's book *Lights and Legends,* the original bell was replaced by a 250-pound bell because of the complaints of nearby residents. Eventually, in 1936, twin diaphragm foghorns were installed.

When the lighthouse was first built, many tons of granite riprap were placed around the caisson for extra protection. An additional 1,200 tons were added between 1891 and 1892. A small oil house and new landing steps were added by 1895.

The first keeper was Frank W. Parmele, who stayed for four years before moving to Rhode Island's Castle Hill Light. Few keepers lasted more than a year or two at Saybrook Breakwater because of the harsh conditions. Strong winds and swift currents frequently made the trip to shore daunting. Flat stones were eventually added to the breakwater, making it possible to walk to the lighthouse, but the sea washed over the rocks and in the winter the breakwater was often covered with ice.

John D. Skipworth, a native of England and previously keeper at Fire Island Light, New York, was keeper from 1890 to 1896. In May 1896 a curious article with the title "A Lighthouse Keeper's Story" appeared in the *New York Times.*

John D. Skipworth, keeper of the new light on the end of the jetty at Saybrook Point, says that on Sunday afternoon, May 10, he sighted from the light a monstrous sea serpent sporting on the surface of the Sound.

He estimates that the serpent measured 300 feet. It had a monstrous head, which it raised occasionally several feet above the rest of its body, and again spouted water in the air like a whale to the height of ten to fifteen feet. The serpent seemed to have an immense body, and judging from what was visible above the water, Keeper Skipworth says it must have been ten or twelve feet in diameter half way between head and tail.

The monster was clearly marked with spots and stripes, and at times resembled the hull of a down-turned yacht. It was headed for the light, and disappeared in the west. The time that it was visible was short.

People laugh at the story, but Mr. Skipworth is undoubtedly in earnest in the matter. He hurried over to the point early yesterday morning, and told what he had seen. He does not ask anybody to believe the story who is inclined to doubt it.

Mr. Skipworth has witnesses to corroborate his story. One of these, he says is the Captain of the schooner Emma, *now unloading at Chester. The Captain's return to these waters is anxiously awaited.*

The keeper's wife was with him in the light, and is another witness to the truth of the story.

This was one of countless reported sightings of sea serpents along the east coast of the United States in the nineteenth century. But the size of the creature described by Skipworth puts it closer to the realm of Japanese science fiction than to the average sighting. It's not known if it had anything to do with the sea serpent scare or suspicious glances from townspeople who had heard his tale, but Skipworth left Saybrook Breakwater three months later.

Another early keeper was John Dahlman, who stayed from 1899 to 1907. One day Dahlman was climbing into the station's boat with his shotgun, intending to go duck hunting. The gun discharged, lacerating the keeper's left arm from the wrist to the elbow. His wife repeatedly sounded the fog bell until it got the attention of the keeper at Lynde Point. A doctor was summoned, and Dahlman eventually recovered.

Herbert S. Knowles was the next keeper. Soon after they arrived in 1907, Knowles and his wife had a son, Russell, born at the lighthouse. Decades later, in 1980, Russell Knowles shared some of his childhood memories with a newspaper reporter:

It used to be a big deal when the whole family would load up the boat and go into town. My mother would put my sister in the baby carriage and my father would push the carriage down the gangplank and into the boat. Once when we were getting ready to go, I was waiting for my parents who were getting my sister dressed up inside the house. The baby carriage was sitting empty at the top of the ramp, and I decided to push the carriage into the boat as I had seen my father do so many times. Well, I ended up pushing the carriage into the water and my mother was so upset that her, my sister and I all moved to a conventional house on what is now Cottage Street—my mother decided that a lighthouse was no place for kids.

The Knowles family left the lighthouse in 1911 and moved to Ohio a few years later. But when he returned for a visit in 1980, Russell looked in the water by the lighthouse just in case he might catch sight of an Ingersoll pocket watch he had dropped there as a small boy. "I watched that old Ingersoll float to the bottom and it made me really sad to lose it," he said. "I haven't owned a watch since."

There were recurring battles over whether an assistant keeper was needed at the station. Dahlman had an assistant, but Knowles did not. In 1917 Keeper Joseph Woods begged for an assistant, saying that his wife, who was ill, was forced to stand watch over the light and fog signal while he rested. But it took a few more years before an assistant was again assigned to the station.

The great hurricane of September 21, 1938, struck New England's south-facing coast with unprecedented fury. The worst damage was along the coast farther east, where the seas rolled in without being obstructed by Long Island. But the storm was a nightmare all along the Connecticut coast. At Saybrook Breakwater Light, the logbook entries of Keeper Sidney Gross describing the storm, reproduced in Hans Christian Adamson's 1955 book, *Keepers of the Lights*, were thankfully detailed and vivid:

At 2 p.m. on the afternoon of September 21 a light southeast breeze sprang up from a perfect calm. At 2:15 p.m. it became so hazy that it was necessary to start sounding the fog signal. By 3 p.m. it was blowing a gale, and I was unable to step outside the engine room door, the only door through which we can enter or leave the building. I made several attempts to get outside to save some of the small articles on the platform, part of them not being lashed down, but I found it impossible, as the wind pushed me right back into the engine room. Assistant Keeper Bennett also made an attempt to get out and save

Saybrook Breakwater Light's foghorns, which were kept busy during the hurricane of 1938. *U.S. Coast Guard photo from 1945.*

some of the gasoline for the engines, but the velocity of the wind had been increasing every minute, and we were absolutely helpless as far as saving anything outside the tower was concerned.

The tide was coming in, and the water in Long Island Sound and the Connecticut River was becoming rougher every minute. The fog signal was being sounded continuously. At 3:30 p.m. the water level almost reached the platform, and at that time the gasoline drum and the bridge to the breakwater were carried away. The wind then shifted from the southeast to the southwest, and the water pounded away still harder. At 4 p.m. the platform encircling the outside of the tower was torn from its fastenings and carried away with everything on it, including the 12-foot rowboat.

By this time the water was so high outside that it backed into the cistern through the overflow pipe, spoiling all our drinking water. Dozens of rocks, weighing several tons, were carried away from the breakwater and from around the tower. Some of them were moved as much as 60 feet from their original locations. The wind was so strong that it carried away the tops of the combers in a spray, so that we could hardly see more than 25 or 30 feet from the station. At 4:30 p.m., the 1,500-gallon oil tank, which was full of kerosene, was carried away. At almost the same time, the 600-gallon oil tank was lifted out of its cradle and carried away.

At 5 p.m. the water level was about even with the deck, just a few inches below the engine room floor. As the wind shifted the waves started to pound at the two fog horns and the south window of the engine room. Assistant Keeper Bennett and myself boarded up the inside of the window as best we could, but at 5 p.m. the waves were pounding so hard that all the glass was smashed in and the boards torn out. We made other attempts to board up the opening, but the water was too powerful. During these efforts a great wave came through the window, carrying the sash and board with it.

I could not ring the bell, as it was impossible to get out on the bell deck; if I had gotten out, I would have been promptly swept overboard. At sunset I disconnected the electric light fixtures, and installed the incandescent oil vapor lamp. The lens was shaking so badly I expected it to fall off the pedestal and break to pieces. I started up the oil vapor lamp, but the mantles collapsed from the vibration as soon as they were put in place. I then removed the oil vapor lamp and put in the fourth order oil wick lamp. The vibration was so great and the draft from the wind so strong that I had to stay up there with the light the whole night to see that it did not smoke up or go out altogether.

At 6 p.m. the water was pouring in through the second-story window into the hall. I boarded up the window with the doors of a small cabinet and what loose material I could find. At this time I could hear the battery house being broken up. Seven of the batteries and my outboard motor were carried away. Everything outside the building was now carried away, and I certainly did not expect to see another sunrise as the whole structure was shaking under the violent pounding. When daylight came at last, what we saw seemed more dream than reality. There was nothing around the tower. Everything was gone except the battery house and even that was badly out of shape.

At the mouth of the Narragansett Bay in Rhode Island, the hurricane demolished a similar cast-iron caisson lighthouse at Whale Rock, taking the life of an assistant keeper with it. About 700 people died in the storm in New England, including seven at lighthouse stations. As the storm grew in intensity, few boats remained on the water, and those that were caught in the gale were beyond the help of a lighthouse. But it was simply the duty of keepers like Sidney Gross and his assistant to keep the light burning, no matter what.

Saybrook Breakwater Light in October 2004. *Photo by the author.*

Tom Buckridge, son of Lynde Point and Montauk Point Keeper John Ninde Buckridge, was keeper at Saybrook Breakwater from February 1942 until late November 1943, when he retired. Many years earlier he had served as an unpaid assistant to his aging father at Lynde Point. After working as a boat builder, factory worker, and fisherman for about 20 years, Tom Buckridge entered the Lighthouse Service and served at New York's Execution Rocks, Race Rock, and Montauk Point lights, followed by the move to Saybrook Breakwater Light. During his time at the breakwater light, Tom's wife, Sarah, lived at their home in Essex, Connecticut, seeing her husband only a few days each month.

Saybrook Breakwater Light was automated in 1959, and Coast Guard personnel at Lynde Point started standing watch at the breakwater light only in bad weather. The Coast Guard completed $64,000 in renovations in 1996, including exterior painting and the removal of a 500-gallon fuel tank. The lighthouse, although boarded up and missing some earlier components, remains a popular icon of the Connecticut coast. In 1993 the state put a portrait of the lighthouse by J. H. Torrance Downs on a special Long Island Sound license plate.

Despite this lighthouse's popularity, the general public isn't permitted to cut across private property or to drive down the small road marked "private" that leads to Lynde Point, so most have to be content with distant views. But you can get a great view from the occasional lighthouse cruises leaving Captain John's Sport Fishing Center in Waterford, Connecticut. Call (860) 443-7259 or visit www.sunbeamfleet.com for details. Camelot Cruises in Haddam, Connecticut, also offers cruises that pass near the lighthouse; see www.camelotcruises.com or call (800) 522-7463.

CHAPTER 18

New London Harbor Light in 1997. ***Photo by the author.***

New London Harbor Light

1761, 1801

The graceful, white, octagonal tower on New London's Pequot Avenue is a nostalgic counterpoint to its younger, more architecturally flashy offshore neighbor, New London Ledge Light. New London Harbor Light is Connecticut's oldest and tallest lighthouse, and it stands as an emblem of the period when New London was one of the busiest ports of the young nation. The city, with its protected harbor at the mouth of the Thames River, recovered from Benedict Arnold's devastating 1781 raid to grow into the third-busiest whaling port in America by the mid-nineteenth century, behind only Nantucket and New Bedford.

According to the 1852 *History of New London, Connecticut,* by Frances Manwaring Caulkins, there was some kind of navigational aid at the entrance to the harbor as early as 1750, but no description survives. Caulkins also informs us that the "beautiful beach along the mouth of the river, north of the light-house, was for many years used as a kind of quarantine ground." It seems that in the 1750s vessels continually arrived with crew members infected with smallpox.

Connecticut's colonial assembly soon determined that a lighthouse was needed, and passed an act in October 1760 that provided for a committee to "affix the place whereon to erect the said Light-House . . . and to procure a suitable person constantly to look after and tend the light and procure oil for the lamps in the said light-house."

Lotteries were then a popular means of fund-raising for construction projects. In 1761, thousands of lottery tickets were sold to raise the needed funds for the lighthouse. After 12 percent was deducted to defray costs and pay the lottery managers, the rest of the proceeds went for construction.

That same year a 64-foot stone tower with a wooden lantern was built on the harbor's west side. This lighthouse, only the fourth to be built in the American colonies, was 24 feet in diameter with walls four feet thick at its base. One of the tower's builders was Rev. Eliphalet Adams, a goldsmith and pastor of New London's First Congregational Church.

The lighthouse was built on land sold to the government by Nathaniel Shaw Jr. (1735–1782) of New London. Shaw's wife, Lucretia, had inherited the land as the only child of Daniel Harris, whose family had lived there for many years. In 1771 Nathaniel Shaw Jr. petitioned the General Assembly, complaining that he was the "sole director, [and] provider for the light-house . . . and that he was obliged to expend of his own money, in that business about twenty pounds." Shaw was repaid for his expenses in 1774, and a shipping tax increase was instituted to cover the ongoing expense of the lighthouse.

In 1790 the lighthouse was ceded to the federal government along with "certain rocks and ledges off against the harbor of New London, called Race Rock, Black Ledge, and Goshen Reef, together with buoys." During the following year, merchant Nathaniel Richards of New London signed a contract with President Washington, agreeing to furnish the lighthouse with "strained Sperm Ceti oil, Cotton Wick, Candles & Soap sufficient to maintain as good a light as has been kept in the said House the Year past . . . the said Light consisting of three lamps of three Spouts each, required annually 800 Gall strained Sperm Ceti oil at 42 cents per galln."

By the turn of the nineteenth century, the lighthouse tower developed a 10-foot crack extending down from its wooden lantern. There were also complaints that the light was blocked from the west by a point of land. Congress appropriated $15,700 for a new tower, and New Londoner Abisha Woodward won the contract to "build the Light House at this place with the Oil Vault and Cisterns for the same and Eclipser and furnish all the materials." The eclipser, a screen that revolved around the light, represented an effort to make the new light stand apart from nearby lights by giving it a flashing characteristic. This equipment was still an innovation; the first eclipser in the United States had been installed in 1797 at Cape Cod's Highland Light.

A woodworker, stonemason, and veteran of the American Revolution, Woodward had previously built the 1793 Bald Head Island Lighthouse in North Carolina and would soon build a stone lighthouse tower on Connecticut's Faulkner's Island. The new 89-foot octagonal brownstone tower at New London was completed in the spring of 1801.

At the request of Commander Stephen Decatur, the light was darkened during the War of 1812. A militia regiment was stationed nearby, and British forces made no attempt to raid or damage the lighthouse despite their blockade of Long Island Sound.

In 1816 the lighthouse received a new set of oil lamps and accompanying reflectors. The year 1833 was one of major changes as contractor Charles H. Smith installed a new iron lantern, copper dome and vane, a new flight of wooden stairs, and a new outer door, among other improvements. The stairway installed that year was replaced by the present iron stairs in 1863.

An 1838 report by Lt. George M. Bache of the U.S. Navy described the current lighting apparatus:

> *Ten lamps, with parabolic reflectors, disposed around two horizontal tables. . . . The reflectors are thirteen inches in diameter, and average in weight 2 lbs. 9 oz. Each one is firmly supported in its place by an iron bracket which is attached to the table. This apparatus was furnished in 1834, and is now in very good order. . . . The lightkeeper covers the ordinary wicks with small pieces of cotton cloth, which he thinks increases the consumption of oil, and causes the lamps to give a brighter light.*

An 1850 inspection described the lighting equipment as being in poor condition: "Lighting chandelier is out of order; several of the arms to the reflector were off and loose, and we were unable to repair them, not having the materials therefor." In 1857 a new fourth-order Fresnel lens from the Henry-LePaute Company in Paris was installed, and that lens remains in use today. It's one of only two classical Fresnel lenses still active in the state's lighthouses.

A new keeper's dwelling was built to the west of the tower in 1818, and a one-story kitchen wing was added years later. That house was replaced by the current brick dwelling in 1863, which had a second floor added for an assistant keeper and his family in 1900.

This light station was the scene of many experiments with fog signals, including various Daboll trumpets and accompanying equipment. In 1873 the Lighthouse Board reported, "Fog signal was in use 282½ hours but the duration of fog was greater, for the former signal was out of repair." A new second-class Daboll trumpet was installed in duplicate.

That signal was in operation for 553 hours in 1874, and 1,165 hours—or an average of more than three hours per day—three years later. In 1883 it was upgraded to a first-class signal. In 1896 a pair of 3.5-horsepower Hornsby-Akroyd oil engines and air compressors were installed to operate the fog trumpets. During 1903 and 1904 a new fog signal building was constructed to make room for new 13-horsepower engines. The city's water supply was extended to the station at the same time.

Local residents complained of the siren's "horrible groaning and shrieking," and the mayor of New London was among 75 people who signed a petition to have the signal silenced. The well-respected Capt. T. A. Scott argued on behalf of the mariners who greatly appreciated the improved signal. A new, slightly less offensive horn was installed a couple of years later, but it must have been a relief to the long-suffering neighbors when the fog signal was relocated to New London Ledge Light offshore on September 5, 1911.

A 1904 article called "Signals of the Sea" by Arthur Hewitt in the magazine *The Outlook* described a visit when the fog signal was still in operation. The keeper he describes is apparently Charles B. Field, who had been there since 1889.

> *The keeper, a Swede, was a very intelligent man; curious to relate, he was a connoisseur in violins, about which he told me a great deal and tried to tell me more; but I wanted to know of other things — the sea and ships.*
>
> *When we were in the tower talking of fog, he told me how one night, when he was operating the horn, and "the fog was so thick yer could have cut it with a knife and it fairly stuck in yer throat," suddenly the sound seemed to strike something and reverberate with a strange echo against the lighthouse. Instinct told him that this was caused by the sails of some ship quite near by and in immediate danger of running on the rocks. He shouted a warning to the invisible ship, and between the blasts of the horn surely enough there came back an answer. He had altered the vessel's course just in time.*

On July 20, 1912, about three years after New London Ledge began service offshore, the light was converted to automatic acetylene gas operation and the keeper was removed. The station had been divided

New London Harbor Light in the early 1900s. *Courtesy of Jim Streeter.*

New London Harbor Light's still-active fourth-order Fresnel lens in 2003. *Photo by the author.*

in two by the arrival of Pequot Avenue around 1868, and the two properties were sold at auction. The light station property, other than the tower itself, was sold for $7,500 and remains in private hands today. It's been in the same family since 1929.

Like all lighthouses in the United States, New London Harbor Light came under Coast Guard control in 1939. In the spring of 2002 the crew of the U.S. Coast Guard cutter *Penobscot Bay*, homeported in Bayonne, New Jersey, paid a visit to New London to scrape and repaint the lighthouse. This required some of the crew to work in buckets hanging on the side of the tower. "I'm not scared of heights," Seaman Michael Davidson told the *New London Day*, "but I am scared of falling."

In May 2003 it was announced by the General Services Administration that New London Harbor Lighthouse had been determined by the Coast Guard to be excess federal property, and that it would be transferred to a new owner under the National Historic Lighthouse Preservation Act of 2000. The New London Maritime Society applied for ownership, and in April 2005 the society was confirmed as the new steward. The New London Maritime Society is also the custodian of the city's 1833 U.S. Customs House, which it manages as the Custom House Maritime Museum. The Coast Guard will continue to maintain the active light. In 2004 the Coast Guard renewed all the trim in the lantern.

Visiting New London Harbor Light is problematic, as the keeper's house and grounds are private property, although there has been discussion regarding some kind of future limited public access. You can see the lighthouse from the sidewalk outside the property on Pequot Avenue, but some of the best views are available from scenic cruises in the area. The periodic lighthouse cruises leaving Captain John's Sport Fishing Center in Waterford, Connecticut, provide an excellent photo opportunity. Call (860) 443-7259 or visit www.sunbeamfleet.com for details.

New London Ledge Light in 2003. *Photo by the author.*

New London Ledge Light

1909

New London Ledge Light is one of the few lighthouses in the United States that can accurately be called one of a kind. There's nothing else like this striking red brick mansion with a lantern on top, rising improbably from the water at the mouth of the Thames River. Its colorful history and legends measure up to its architecture.

Officials were concerned with obstructions at the mouth of the Thames River near New London's harbor as early as 1794. On March 20 of that year the House of Representatives resolved:

> *That the Secretary of the Treasury be authorized and directed to cause to be fixed on the rocks called Blackledge, or Southwest ledge, Goshen reef, Bartlet's reef, and Race rock, off the harbor of New London, in the State of Connecticut, four buoys, at an expense not to exceed twelve hundred dollars.*

In 1845 citizens petitioned Congress for a lighthouse on Black Ledge. And again in 1854 masters of vessels, pilots, and others petitioned for a beacon in the same location. In 1865 they asked for a lightship. The plea for a lighthouse again went out in 1890, but only a buoy would mark the area for two more decades.

New London's days as one of the nation's leading whaling ports were long past by the late nineteenth century, but the city made a smooth transition into a center of manufacturing and industry. In addition, a U.S. Navy yard (which would later become a submarine base) had been established in Groton, on the east bank of the Thames River. Frank B. Brandegee, a senator and a native of New London, was a catalyst in the push for improved local navigational aids.

The Lighthouse Board, in its annual reports for 1902 and 1903, asked Congress for an appropriation of $60,000 for a lighthouse. George B. Cortelyou of the board wrote:

> *The necessity for establishing a light and an efficient fog signal in such a position as to enable vessels to enter and leave the harbor of New London, Conn., has become evident, and especially so for the aid of those approaching from seaward.*

The numerous outlying shoals and ledges surrounding the entrance to this harbor make the approach to it dangerous in thick weather. The location of the present New London light and fog-signal station is so far inside the obstructions as to be partially ineffective as an aid for the purpose of safe navigation of this entrance. The commerce of the port of New London has so increased since the erection of the present light as to change the conditions materially.

Black Ledge was considered as a site for the new lighthouse, but that would have left Southwest Ledge as a dangerous hazard between the lighthouse and the shipping channel, so Southwest Ledge was instead chosen as the site. The lighthouse was at first called Southwest Ledge Light, but to avoid confusion with the lighthouse of the same name in New Haven, it was officially changed in 1910 to New London Ledge Light.

An appropriation of $60,000 for a light and fog signal was authorized in April 1904. Drawings for the lighthouse were prepared in 1906. Additional funds were appropriated, and it was agreed that the new lighthouse would be erected at a cost not exceeding $115,000. The basic design of the structure was a throwback to the combined dwelling-lighthouses of the nineteenth century. This type of construction had mostly been supplanted by the ubiquitous "sparkplug" lighthouses, usually cast-iron, built on cast-iron cylindrical caissons. That style would have been the obvious choice for this location.

Some have suggested that this lighthouse was built in an elegant style largely because nearby wealthy homeowners wanted something that wouldn't look out of place. With its mansard roof and paired windows and doors, the style is often classified as French Second Empire. But it also reflects the influence of Colonial Revival architecture in a variety of features, such as its red-painted brick with white trim.

Work began in July 1908 on a timber crib that would serve as a form for the foundation. This work was done in Groton by the T. A. Scott Company, a marine salvage and construction company. Captain Thomas Albertson Scott, who started the company, was a renowned diver who was foreman for the underwater work during the building of Race Rock Lighthouse in Fisher's Island Sound. He was the subject of a 1908 book called *Captain Thomas A. Scott, Master Diver* by engineer/author Francis Hopkinson Smith.

The crib was made of 162,000 feet of southern yellow pine held together with nine tons of steel and iron; it was large enough to hold 3,500 barrels of concrete. On July 20 the partially finished crib was towed three miles and put into position. It took four tugboats eight hours to complete the tow. The tenders *Iris* and *Mistletoe* were on hand, and their crews removed the buoys that marked the ledge.

The crib was completed while still afloat and was then sunk into the water. It was filled with concrete, gravel, and riprap and topped by a three-foot layer of concrete. The finished foundation was about 35 feet high and 52 feet square. Granite riprap, about 10 feet deep and 82 feet square, was added for extra protection around the foundation. The timber crib was removed in 1938 and a new boarding edge was added around the perimeter.

Work was halted by winter but resumed early in 1909. A concrete pier, 50 feet square and rising 18 feet above low water, was added on top of the foundation, with space cut out to serve as a basement. Atop the pier the lighthouse superstructure, 32 feet square and 34 feet 6 inches high, was constructed. The subcontractor for the building of the three-story lighthouse was the Hamilton R. Douglas Company, the same company that built the town hall in Groton.

A cylindrical cast-iron lantern surmounted an octagonal brick watchroom on the center of the roof. A fourth-order Fresnel lens manufactured by the Henry-LePaute Company of Paris was installed, displaying three white flashes followed by a red flash every 30 seconds, with a focal plane 58 feet above mean high water. The lens rotated with the help of weights and a clockwork mechanism that had to be wound every 10 to 14 hours.

The station went into operation on November 10, 1909, and was assigned a principal keeper and two assistants. Its final cost was $93,968.96.

Navigators were in agreement that the new light was a valuable addition. Captain Samuel Crocker, a longtime local captain, was quoted in the *New London Day* a day after the light went into operation.

> *It's a nice light and a good deal of an improvement. We saw it flash when we were westward of Cornfield lightship. We could easily tell where the rocks are. . . . The light is going to be a great help in starting out from New London as we can steer almost straight for it.*

A first-class fog siren was also installed, powered by compressed air and gasoline engines. Playwright Eugene O'Neill lived on Pequot Avenue in New London for many years. His semiautobiographical play *Long Day's Journey into Night* was set there in 1912, and his characters apparently refer to the fog signal at New London Ledge in one section of the play. It's also possible that O'Neill was thinking of the older, piercing signal at New London Harbor Light. Perhaps he was voicing his own feelings through his character Mary Tyrone in the following exchange:

Mary: That foghorn! Isn't it awful, Cathleen?
Cathleen: It is indeed, Ma'am. It's like a banshee.
Mary: I don't mind it tonight. Last night it drove me crazy. I lay awake worrying until I couldn't stand it any more. . . . It's the foghorn I hate. It won't let you alone. It keeps reminding you, and warning you, and calling you back. But it can't tonight. It's just an ugly sound. It doesn't remind me of anything.

One of the early head keepers was George Hanson, who had to be rescued by the keeper at North Dumpling Light, New York, on a cold January day in 1913 when his outboard motor failed.

New London native Howard B. Beebe arrived as a second assistant keeper in 1926 and eventually became the head keeper. His daughter, Barbara Gaspar, recalls visiting the lighthouse as a girl. She would fish from the deck around the lighthouse, securely tied by a rope to the railing. She also remembers that at night her mother would send signals from shore using a flashlight, and her father would answer from the lighthouse.

Keeper Beebe was in the lighthouse during the hurricane of 1938, the worst storm of the twentieth century in New England, along with a second assistant keeper and a tinsmith.

"It washed out everything," Beebe recalled in the *Providence Journal* years later. "About 3:15, the engines conked out, but the light was going. We moved to the lantern. It was a three-story building. Waves were coming through the second floor. I've seen waves before, in the Bay of Fundy, but I never saw them like that. There was 11 tons of coal in the cellar, and it boiled it all out."

After the Coast Guard took over the operation of lighthouses in 1939, two- or three-man crews lived at the lighthouse. By the 1980s the crewmen were spending two weeks at the station followed by a week onshore, with Fridays being the exchange day. The crew at that time was mostly very young, between 18 and 33 years old. Wives and girlfriends could visit, but only immediate family was permitted to stay overnight. The men had occasional visits from locals with gifts of fish, lobster, and cold beverages. They kept in touch with shore-dwellers via citizens band radio, and in fact young crewman Richard J. Mumenthaler of Philadelphia met his fiancée over the radio.

When the men weren't keeping 12-hour watches they passed their time swimming, fishing, playing cards, working out in a small gym, taking correspondence courses, or watching soap operas on TV. Life was mostly routine—even boring—except for the occasional rescue of

New London Ledge Light in 1960. *U.S. Coast Guard photo.*

a swimmer or boater. But according to Mumenthaler and many other keepers, the place could be "incredibly spooky" at night.

Strange events were said to be commonplace during this period. Doors opened and closed themselves; the TV turned itself off and on. A deck "swabbed itself." Randy Watkins, officer in charge in the early 1980s, said he once heard his name being called from an upstairs room when the other crewman was asleep. His wife, Lucretia, spent a night in the master bedroom and said she was awakened when the door opened, followed by "the eerie feeling of someone in the room, staring." And one time two fishermen secured their boat and came inside for a visit. The men laughed at talk of a ghost, but stopped laughing when they saw their boat was untied and drifting away.

These and many other odd happenings were invariably attributed to "Ernie," who has become the best-known lighthouse ghost of the Northeast. Author William O. Thomson says that Ernie would turn on the foghorn, polish brass, and clean windows. Actual ghost sightings were rare, and supposedly only visiting women have ever seen the ethereal resident.

The story usually used to explain Ernie's origins follows. There are some variations depending on who's doing the telling, and I make no guarantee that any part of the story is true.

In the 1920s or 1930s a new keeper came to New London Ledge Light. The keeper's true name isn't known, but he was known to all as Ernie. Ernie had a new young wife, half his age, who lived in New London while he stayed at the lighthouse. What started as a happy marriage dissolved into despair and desperation as the young woman pined for a normal life with her husband.

One bleak day Ernie found a letter left by his wife, telling him that she had run off with the captain of the Block Island ferry. The keeper's will to live was crushed. Some say he jumped from the roof of the lighthouse to his death, while others say he drank himself senseless and then accidentally fell to his death. Some claim that he made an oath before his death to avenge himself in some way.

Nobody has uncovered evidence that these events ever occurred, and there's no record of a keeper named Ernie. This seems to be a case of a story being fabricated to explain the unexplainable, or maybe a case of young men with too much time and imagination on their hands. But there may be reasons to believe that this lighthouse has indeed been the scene of paranormal activity.

Dr. Roger Pile, who calls himself a "ghost psychologist," visited the lighthouse along with his wife (who acted as a medium) in December 1981. According to the Piles, the spirit revealed itself to be a keeper named John Randolph. (Once again there are no records of any keeper by this name.) The Piles reported that Randolph had never been married, but he had lost the woman he loved because of a terrible argument. The distraught keeper proceeded to stab himself in the throat and fall from the lighthouse to his death. Pile performed a ritual that was supposed to free Randolph's spirit, and a newspaper soon reported that ghostly activity had ceased—however, a November 1985 article in the *New London Day* disagreed.

The automation and destaffing of New London Ledge Light had been scheduled for 1986, and according to the *New London Day* article the Coast Guard crew claimed that Ernie was agitated over the coming change. Charles Kerr said that papers on his desk rearranged themselves, and Paul Noke's bed moved around his room by itself. Noke eventually started sleeping on a couch after tiring of the moving bed. Only one of the crewmen, Steven Bailey, expressed doubt about Ernie's existence. "If he kicks me out of bed and throws me down the stairs," said Bailey, "I'll leave."

The Coast Guard wanted to find a new tenant to care for the lighthouse before they automated the light and moved out. For about 15 years the crews had given informal tours of the building to school groups and others, and the Coast Guard expressed a desire to find a nonprofit group that would make public access a priority. Various groups expressed interest, including the New London Marine Commerce and Development Committee, the New London Maritime Society, Mystic Seaport, and the New London County Historical Society.

The automation was officially completed on May 1, 1987, making this the last lighthouse on Long Island Sound to be automated. One of the last Coast Guard crewmen painted a portrait of the lighthouse on one of its interior walls.

A nonprofit organization called Project Oceanology soon took a lead role in the lighthouse's future. The group, based at Avery Point in Groton, had already been ferrying students to the lighthouse for tours. Dr. Howard Weiss, director of the organization, envisioned the lighthouse as an educational attraction for school groups, a lighthouse museum for the public, and a platform for marine research.

The Coast Guard eventually issued a 30-year lease to the New London Ledge Lighthouse Foundation, a new nonprofit group comprising residents of Groton, New London, and Waterford as well as local government officials, industry, and Project Oceanology. The New London Ledge Lighthouse Foundation continues to manage the property and has been gradually restoring the building since the late 1980s.

A $100,000 state grant in 1989 paid for some improvements, including a new stairway from the boat landing, a sewage treatment plant, and desalinization equipment. The windows, boarded up when the light was automated, were uncovered. The New London Ledge Lighthouse Foundation's ultimate goal is to establish a museum at the lighthouse and offer overnight stays.

Solar panels were added to the lighthouse in 1998, providing power for the light and fog signal. A cable from Avery Point provides the rest of the electricity. The fourth-order Fresnel lens was removed during the automation process, and eventually went to the Custom House Maritime Museum in New London, where it remains on display. The active optic in the lighthouse is now a rotating VRB-25.

The restoration of New London Ledge Light has progressed at a gradual but steady pace over the years, but there is still much to be done. In August 2003 several volunteers of the New England Lighthouse Lovers (NELL), a chapter of the American Lighthouse Foundation, spent a weekend at the lighthouse scraping and painting the lantern room as well as preparing another room for painting. Jim Streeter of NELL, who has also spearheaded the restoration of nearby Avery Point Lighthouse, wrote the following about the experience:

> *I grew up in Groton and . . . spent many a night sitting on the rocks with my first found love watching the "submarine races." I recall how beautiful and romantic it was to sit and hold this girl in my arms as we watched the light cast its red and white rays of light upon us. . . . I recall how we listened to the deep and recurring sounds of the*

foghorn from the lighthouse. I was fortunate to have married this same teenage love, and over 38 years later we were blessed with the opportunity to give a little of ourselves back to the same lighthouse which meant so much to our relationship.

Stories of unexplainable events continue to emanate from New London Ledge. In the book *Haunted Lighthouses and How to Find Them* by George C. Steitz, Brae Rafferty of the New London Ledge Lighthouse Foundation offered an alternative to the "Ernie" story to explain the origins of the resident ghost or ghosts. Rafferty had met a woman whose grandfather helped build the lighthouse. According to the woman the strange phenomena at the site started before the lighthouse was even completed, with eerie sounds, weird shadows, and tools that vanished during construction.

Rafferty's research showed that there was a shipwreck on Black Ledge about a decade before the lighthouse was built. Many of the dozen or so passengers died, including a newly married young woman. The woman's husband desperately combed the nearby shores but found no sign of his beloved. Witnesses then saw the man walk slowly out into the water toward Black Ledge until he disappeared and drowned. So—if you're inclined to so believe—a spirit may have been already waiting for a place to haunt when the lighthouse was built.

And there's still another story offered to explain the strange goings-on here. According to a brochure produced by Jerry Olson of the New London Ledge Lighthouse Foundation, "It has been said that around 1913–1914, a sailboat departed New Jersey bound for New Bedford." The sailboat passed through Long Island Sound, where it ran into a tremendous storm. Late that night the light keeper looked into the water and saw a man and a woman desperately swimming toward the lighthouse. After helping them ashore, he learned that their sailboat had capsized and they had lost their daughter in the wreck.

Early the next morning the keeper arose and went to check on his guests. To his astonishment he found no trace of the couple. Days later when the seas calmed down and the keeper reached shore, he was told by friends that they had rescued a young woman who said that her parents had been lost in a sailboat wreck. But this woman, too, had mysteriously vanished.

"It has been said," concludes the brochure, "that on particular dark nights, a spirit has been observed roaming the lighthouse searching for a loved one." Over the years people have encountered the spirit and have named her 'The Lady of the Ledge.'" Jerry Olson claims that he has had a personal encounter with this mysterious lady. One day while

Paranormal investigator Christine Kaczynski says that this 2000 photo shows evidence of "supernatural energy" at the lighthouse. The photo was taken with her Olympus automatic 35mm camera using 800-speed film with flash, as she stood at the front steps of the lighthouse looking to the north at the top landing of the docking stairway. *Courtesy of Christine Kaczynski.*

he was alone in the basement of the lighthouse, cleaning the cisterns, Olson says he heard the distinct sound of a woman clearing her throat behind him. He says he immediately had the image of an attractive middle-aged woman in his mind's eye, but upon turning around he saw nothing.

In recent years paranormal investigator Christine Kaczynski has visited the lighthouse on several occasions with assistants and sophisticated equipment including cameras, motion detectors, and an oscilloscope. Kaczynski is a no-nonsense woman who puts no stock in the "Ernie" legend or in Pile's investigation, but she claims her investigations clearly show the lighthouse to be the scene of much spirit activity. She says the third floor is the "vortex" of the activity, and that the northeast corner of the building is the most active. She also says that the spirit or spirits are benign and not at all dangerous, although one person did feel strongly that someone "didn't want them there."

Project Oceanology provides public tours of the lighthouse in season. For details you can call (860) 445-9007 or visit the "Project O" Web site at www.oceanology.org. You can also get a good look from the decks of the New London–Block Island ferry, as well as from the occasional lighthouse cruises leaving Captain John's Sport Fishing Center in Waterford, Connecticut. Call (860) 443-7259 or visit www.sunbeamfleet.com for details. You can also contact the New London Ledge Lighthouse Foundation for more information at P.O. Box 855, New London, CT 06320.

Avery Point Light, circa 1996. *Photo by the author.*

Avery Point Light

1944

This lighthouse's life as an active navigational aid (from 1944 to 1967) was relatively brief, and it never had a resident keeper like its older neighbors. But like every lighthouse, it has its own compelling story. If it could talk, this unique and handsome tower would tell a moving tale of a comeback from the edge of total ruin. And it would no doubt express undying gratitude to its saviors, the tenacious volunteers of the Avery Point Lighthouse Society.

Avery Point Light stands on the shore at the east side of the entrance to the Thames River on the University of Connecticut's Avery Point Campus in Groton. Avery Point is named for Capt. James Avery, a prominent early settler of New London. The campus was once the 70-plus-acre estate of wealthy industrialist, philanthropist, and yachtsman Morton F. Plant.

Plant died in 1918, and in 1942 the estate was sold to the state of Connecticut. Shortly thereafter it was deeded to the U.S. Coast Guard, which planned to develop it into a training facility. The Coast Guard had a small training facility on the New London side of the Thames but needed a larger site. The deed from the state stipulated that the Coast Guard would "erect and maintain on or over the land hereinafter described beacon lights or other buildings and apparatus to be used in aid of navigation."

The United States Coast Guard Training Station was soon established, with Branford House serving as an administration building and living quarters for the station's commanding officer. Thousands of Coast Guard personnel received training at the site.

The lighthouse, the last to be built in Connecticut, was finished by March 1943. Its debut as a lighted aid to navigation was delayed by war concerns. On May 2, 1944, it was lighted for the first time with an unusual array of eight 200-watt bulbs, creating a fixed white light 55 feet above sea level. The light was useful for vessels entering a cove east of Avery Point and for those navigating the Pine Island Channel. The light also served a purpose for keepers at Race Rock Light out in Fisher's Island Sound. When the fog got so thick that they could no longer see the light at Avery Point, the keepers knew it was time to turn the foghorn on.

Avery Point Light in 1945. *National Archives photo.*

The octagonal 41-foot tower, designed by Alfred Hopkins and Associates of New York, New York, harks back to the nation's eighteenth- and nineteenth-century masonry towers and has some Colonial Revival details. It was constructed of light brown concrete blocks with an eight-sided wooden lantern. The lantern gallery deck was surrounded by a cast-concrete railing with 32 white Italian marble balusters salvaged from a garden or terrace on the Plant estate. At the time the tower was built the Coast Guard proclaimed that the balusters and arched windows provided "a touch of Williamsburg." The south-facing side of the tower was given two windows, with three other sides having single windows. The first 17 feet of the interior are open, with a wooden ladder leading to the watchroom level. The wooden ladder was later replaced by an iron one.

In the 1994 edition of his book *America's Atlantic Coast Lighthouses: A Traveler's Guide,* Kenneth Kochel says that "the tower was built as a memorial tower and as a symbolic representation of the USCG lighthouse keeping responsibilities." According to the listing for the National Register of Historic Places prepared by the Connecticut Historical Commission, this "misunderstanding" dates back to a 1955 article in the *U.S. Coast Guard Magazine.* The article, by Robert Miller, stated:

> *When the State of Connecticut gave the Training Station property to the Coast Guard there was one stipulation—"that a light tower be built at the extremity of the peninsula where day and night it would serve as a reminder of illustrious names from the past and an active and useful present." Remember whose names, I don't know, but maybe it's the names of students—like the 1,462 who graduated last year.*

The "illustrious names" could also be interpreted to mean lighthouse keepers of the past. In any event, no such language actually appeared in the deed. Although the origins of the memorial notion are hazy, it's been repeated so often that for all intents and purposes Avery Point Light has come to serve that very purpose for many people.

During its active years, the light was apparently tended by personnel or students from the training facility, saving the expense of a keeper or attendant. In 1960 the light's characteristic was changed to flashing green and the candlepower was increased from 100 to 200.

In 1967 the Coast Guard relocated its training facility from Avery Point to Governor's Island, New York. The lighthouse's days as an aid to navigation ended on June 25, 1967. The Avery Point property reverted to the state of Connecticut, and in 1969 it was converted to the Southeastern Campus of the University of Connecticut, later renamed the University of Connecticut at Avery Point.

The lighthouse was used for a time by Coast Guard research and development personnel for various navigational aid experiments. The University of Connecticut physics department later used it for air quality experiments. But it was eventually abandoned, and the elements and neglect exacted their toll. The concrete blocks were pitted and began to crumble, the wooden lantern rotted, and chunks of the marble balusters fell to the ground. By July 1997 the university said the tower was in "dangerously poor condition" and declared it a safety hazard. In December 1997 it was added to the "Doomsday List" of *Lighthouse Digest.*

Jim Streeter, a state police handwriting expert and former deputy mayor of Groton, spearheaded a drive to save the local landmark. In 1999 fund-raising began through the American Lighthouse Foundation of Wells, Maine, and the following year the Avery Point Lighthouse Society (APLS) was founded as a chapter. Stephen W. Gulyas and Dale Treadway came on board as cochairmen with Streeter. A petition drive eventually garnered the signatures of more than 19,000 people supporting the restoration and relighting of Avery Point Light.

Restoration was first estimated at $150,000, but as time passed it became clear that it could run as high as $350,000 or more. By the fall of 2000, $12,000 had been raised. Many people also chipped in with in-kind donations, such as James Norden of Gibble Norden Champion Consulting Engineers of Old Saybrook, who provided an engineering study of the tower at no cost, and Don Perkins of Cape Cod, who created and donated a finely detailed replica of the lighthouse to be exhibited to raise awareness and donations. The New England Lighthouse Lovers (NELL), another chapter of the American Lighthouse Foundation, donated funds for a new door for the lighthouse.

The University of Connecticut signed a memorandum of agreement to allow the APLS to begin restoration. On December 1, 2001, workers from Mattern Construction of Baltic, Connecticut, and Marino Crane Company of Hartford lifted the lantern off the tower using a 90-foot crane. An elaborate cradle was first constructed around the lantern to prevent damage when it was moved. Because the old lantern was so deteriorated, it was decided that a replica would be made. The old lantern was moved a short distance away to a spot on campus and was later moved to the West Mystic Wooden Boat Building Company's facilities to be used as a template for the replica.

The West Mystic Wooden Boat Building Company fabricated the new lantern in 2003 and 2004, donating the cost of labor and materials. The company is owned by former lighthouse keeper (at Harbor of Refuge Light in Delaware) and University of Connecticut English professor Steve Jones. The new lantern was constructed by Mark C. Robinson, a carpenter and boatbuilder for the company.

In January 2002 the efforts of APLS took a huge leap forward when the Connecticut State Bond Commission approved a $150,000 grant. Another successful fund-raising component has been a "Brick-Buy-Brick" campaign. As of September 2004, over 2,000 personalized bricks have been sold at $50 each, and they will eventually become part of a landscaped walkway and apron around the tower.

Examination of the tower's crumbling concrete blocks revealed that they had been fabricated using a high amount of sand. As the mortar between the blocks expanded and contracted over the years, the poorly made blocks began to crumble. It was decided that the only way to save the tower would be to remove the outer faces of the blocks and replace them with new block faces. At the same time the old blocks would be strengthened with cement and steel reinforcements.

At one point, APLS was abruptly notified that additional funds were needed before work could begin, and they didn't have enough on hand. Time was of the essence, and the Cape Cod Chapter of the American Lighthouse Foundation came through with a donation of $25,000. Phase One of the restoration, the replacement of the block faces, was completed in 2003 at a cost of over $200,000.

Meanwhile, it was determined that the rest of the restoration would cost more than initially thought. On November 3, 2003, Rep. Rob Simmons met with members of APLS and the university at the lighthouse to announce that $100,000 in federal funding would be granted for the project under the Save America's Treasures program.

Jim Streeter said in the fall of 2004 that with unanticipated expenses and inflation, the group still needed to raise approximately $25,000 to $50,000 for restoration. The plan is eventually to create a museum in the bottom floor of the tower. There are also plans to

The old lantern room (left) and the new replica lantern room created and donated by the West Mystic Wooden Boat Building Company. *Photos by Ron Foster.*

install benches near the water near the new brick walkway, looking out at New London Ledge Light and other sights in Fisher's Island Sound and Long Island Sound.

APLS would also like to work with the groups involved with New London Ledge and New London Harbor lights to create a sort of "Connecticut Three Sisters Lights" tourism venture. "Once you get the lighthouse restoration bug," says Streeter, "you want to direct your energies to saving and restoring other historic lighthouses."

To visit Avery Point Lighthouse, take I-95 north or south to Exit 87 onto CT 349 (Clarence B. Sharp Highway). Continue on CT 349 and turn right at the second traffic light. At the next traffic light, turn left onto Benham Road (still CT 349) and proceed for about 1.5 miles. Where the road curves sharply left, CT 349 ends and the road changes names to Shennecossett Road. Here there is an entrance to the University of Connecticut at Avery Point. After entering the property, continue driving straight back toward the water. Follow the circular drive past the police station and park anywhere in the visitor parking areas. Walk across the field, heading east (away from the river and past the library). The lighthouse is about 500 feet from the circular drive.

The restored Avery Point Lighthouse will be dedicated in a ceremony sometime in September 2005. To learn more you can visit the APLS Web site at www.averypointlight.com or write to Avery Point Lighthouse Society, P.O. Box 1552, Groton, CT 06340.

CHAPTER 21

Morgan Point Light in 2002. *Photo by the author.*

21

Morgan Point Light

1831, 1868

Noank, a village of the town of Groton, was a thriving center for shipbuilding and fishing in the nineteenth century. Lobstering has long been a big business here. In fact, it's claimed that in the 1890s Noank supplied half the lobster catch for the entire state. Historian Charles R. Stark wrote in 1922 that Noank "has always maintained a high moral and religious standard, the open sale of intoxicants has never been tolerated, poverty is almost unknown and the neighborly friendship existing is ideal." Despite casinos a short drive away and touristy Mystic just up the road, Noank—which is said to get its name from a Mohegan Indian word for "point"—remains a charming, unspoiled New England maritime village.

When ownership of the peninsula was divided up in 1712, Noank's southern tip at the west side of the entrance to the Mystic River was allotted to Deacon James Morgan. His descendants were seafarers and shipbuilders, and it was his great-great-grandson Roswell Avery Morgan, owner of the Morgan boat shop, who sold the point to the federal government for the building of a lighthouse in 1831. Congress had appropriated $5,000 for the station, and a 25-foot round granite tower and a six-room keeper's dwelling were constructed for $4,148.43.

W. Crawford, a customs collector in New London and local lighthouse superintendent, wrote in an 1837 letter that the lighthouse had been "built under the constant inspection of Mr. Ezra Daboll, a practical mechanic and house builder, who had no share in the profit or loss resulting from the contract. . . . He certified that the work had been faithfully done. I also inspected it personally, and frequently, during its progress, and was satisfied with the builder's performance of his contract."

Ezra Daboll, a veteran of the War of 1812, was appointed the first keeper of the light. Daboll died in 1838 at the age of 53 and left his widow, Eliza Ledyard Daboll, with six children. Eliza won the appointment to replace her husband as keeper. In his book *Lights and Legends*, Harlan Hamilton informs us that Eliza's eldest daughter helped tend the light and that, according to legend, passing sailors often heard her singing loudly to keep her courage up during storms.

Eliza remained keeper at Morgan Point until 1854. In an 1838 report, Lt. George M. Bache of the U.S. Navy wrote, "The establishment is kept with great neatness by the widow of the former keeper."

Lieutenant Bache reserved his criticism for the lighting apparatus in his 1838 report. The 10 lamps and 13-inch parabolic reflectors, he said, were "out of order." He added that "the silver is rubbed from their [reflectors'] concave surfaces in many places" and that the light was barely visible two and a half miles away.

An 1850 inspection again praised Eliza Daboll's housekeeping but was critical of other aspects:

> *The light-house, I will say, is in good order, with one or two trifling exceptions. Dwelling, which is part of wood and part of stone, needs a few trifling repairs, as window-shutters and cellar-door frame to keep the cold from the cellar. Mrs. Daboll thinks the house ought to be painted. The lantern ought to be painted inside and out. I found one part of the sills to the house very much decayed, but perhaps not sufficiently so to require new sills, and to require them immediately. Everything about the dwelling is nice and clean, but not so with the lighting apparatus, for that, as a general thing, is not near so clean as it ought to be. Spent a considerable time in adjusting and repairing the apparatus.*

The 1855 Annual Report of the Lighthouse Board announced that a sixth-order steamer lens and Argand lamp had replaced the old lamps and reflectors. Further improvements came with the construction of a new combination lighthouse and dwelling in 1867 at a cost of $11,719.19. Henry Davis, who lived on Pearl Street in Noank, was the contractor in charge.

The new lighthouse, completed in 1868, was a two-story, eight-room structure of native granite with a cast-iron light tower attached to the front of the building, its focal plane 61 feet above the ocean. The style of the building was similar to several others built in the same period, including Connecticut's Sheffield Island and Great Captain Island lights, New York's Plum Island and Old Field Point lights, and Rhode Island's Block Island North Light. The old buildings were removed, except for a wooden addition to the earlier dwelling that was converted into a stable. In 1869 the Lighthouse Board reported that "this station is now in excellent order and good condition, and the keeper takes good care of everything at the station."

The first keeper of the new lighthouse was Alexander McDonald, a former ship's carpenter originally from Prince Edward Island, who came to Morgan Point in 1867. McDonald had never fully recovered

Nineteenth-century photo of Morgan Point Light.
Courtesy of James W. Claflin.

from his confinement in Danville Prison during the Civil War, and in 1869 his ill health prompted him to move to Florida. His wife, Frances Pecor McDonald, stayed behind as keeper at Morgan Point until 1871, when she, too, went south and became assistant keeper to her husband at Florida's St. John's River Lighthouse. More than a decade later, after her husband's death, Frances returned to Mystic.

At Morgan Point, Frances McDonald was replaced as keeper by her brother, Thaddeus Pecor, a Mystic native and Civil War veteran who would serve a remarkable 48 years at the lighthouse. Pecor, who was born in Mystic in 1844, had first gone to sea at the age of 14 aboard a fishing smack out of Noank. His fishing career was interrupted by three years of service in the Civil War, mostly in Virginia.

Following the war Pecor worked at shipyards in Mystic and Noank until his appointment as keeper on November 22, 1871. That first winter remained unusually warm into January, when it turned stormy and cold. Before the winter was over, three shipwrecks had come ashore nearby.

An 1899 article in the *New London Day* sang the praises of Keeper Pecor, who had then been at the light for 28 years, at the time the longest stint of any keeper in the district.

> *In that length of time Mr. Pecor has never failed to ascend to the light each night promptly at 12 o'clock to ascertain its condition, nor has he been absent from duty a day with the exception of four days leave of absence, which was granted him by the secretary of the treasury, to attend the national convention of the Grand Army at Washington a few years ago. More than this, the light has never been extinguished between the hours of sunset and sunrise during that time, so attentive has Mr. Pecor been to his duty.*

Another article appeared in the *Day* on the occasion of Pecor's retirement in April 1919, when he was 75 years old.

> *Mr. Pecor has been ably assisted in the duties of lighthouse work by his wife, who was Miss [Sarah] Ann Swaney. They were married 49 years ago. The couple have one son, Frank, and three grandchildren, all of whom make their home with them and share with assisting them down the sunny slope of life. . . .*
>
> *Mr. Pecor has the reputation of keeping the best lighthouse along the coast and he and his wife will both be greatly missed from the village. He always had a smile and pleasant word for those he met and friends and strangers alike were made welcome at his home.*

Just two years after the Pecors left Morgan Point, the old lighthouse was extinguished. Its replacement was a gas-powered automatic light added atop a granite daymarker, known as Crook's Beacon, at the mouth of the river. The new light went into operation on August 15, 1921. Today a small steel skeleton tower with an electric green light marks the spot. In 1922 the lighthouse, after its lantern had been removed, was sold at auction to a couple named Huett, who in turn sold it to Woodruff and Kay Johnson in 1965.

When the most devastating New England storm of the twentieth century, the great hurricane of 1938, struck Noank, neighborhood residents headed for cover inside the sturdy old lighthouse. They believed it was the safest place to be, and they were proved right as the building survived the storm unscathed.

As a young boy in Greenwich, Connecticut, Jason Pilalas loved Great Captain Island Lighthouse and would sometimes row out to visit its Coast Guard keepers. A few decades later in 1991, Pilalas, an investment analyst who mostly lives in San Marino, California, was visiting friends in Rhode Island when a tiny real estate ad caught his eye. The ad showed a lighthouse for sale, one that was practically a twin of the one he had known in

The lighthouse got a new lantern in the 1990s, courtesy of the Pilalases. *Courtesy of Jason and Rena Pilalas.*

Greenwich. Before long Jason and his wife, Rena, were the proud owners of the Morgan Point Lighthouse.

With the help of Herman Hassinger Architects and Octagram Construction of New Jersey, the Pilalases had the exterior of the lighthouse restored to its former appearance; the interior was adapted into a practical, comfortable, and bright living and working space. The interior, which had largely fallen into disrepair, was gutted to the granite walls and reconfigured. Herman Hassinger designed a major addition to the rear of the building that encompasses a great room, master bedroom, guest suite, kitchen, and office. The 1868 lighthouse became the children's wing, with a library and living area on the first floor and bedrooms on the second floor.

To top off the building's rebirth, a new lantern was fabricated to top the tower. The octagonal lantern is based on original Lighthouse Service designs, but it was constructed of aluminum by Atlantic Towers, a Rhode Island company. It was made slightly larger than the original so that it could serve as a sitting room with a spectacular view, the perfect place for a cocktail at sunset.

The first floor interior of the lighthouse is neatly filled with Jason Pilalas's amazing collection of naval antiques, many from the United Kingdom. Among other curiosities, bells from ships of the Royal Navy are displayed alongside a plaque dedicated to the musicians of the band lost on the *Titanic.*

Relatives of the previous owners spoke of the "friendly ghost" of Thaddeus Pecor, claiming that he mysteriously closed doors upstairs while all the residents were downstairs. Rena and Jason Pilalas have yet to experience any apparitions, although they do say that visitors on two separate occasions reported seeing the ghostly form of an old sea captain or keeper.

The Pilalases cherish the time they spend at the lighthouse. They spent more than $1 million for the property and close to that amount to renovate it, but to them it was apparently worth every penny. Jason has been known to fire a 10-gauge cannon to entertain passing tour boat passengers, and the lighthouse is the scene of a yearly gathering of family and friends around the Fourth of July. Rena told *Coastal Living* magazine, "They sleep on couches, they sleep on the floor. They don't care—they just like being here."

The general public can't visit this privately owned lighthouse and its grounds, but excellent views are available from occasional lighthouse cruises leaving Captain John's Sport Fishing Center in Waterford, Connecticut. Call (860) 443-7259 or visit www.sunbeamfleet.com for details.

Stonington Harbor Lighthouse in January 2004. *Photo by the author.*

Stonington Harbor Light

1824, 1840

This rather austere-looking stone lighthouse is tucked away in the southeast corner of Connecticut, at the foot of Water Street in the compact, picturesque old borough of Stonington. Stonington Harbor Light is the only lighthouse on the mainland in Connecticut open to the public on a regular basis. The fortress-like exterior belies the warm and inviting atmosphere inside the Old Lighthouse Museum run by the Stonington Historical Society. It's a real gem for anyone interested in the colorful past of this area.

Stonington boasts many beautiful eighteenth- and nineteenth-century buildings and a rich history dating back to the mid-seventeenth century, when it was first settled. One of the most celebrated events in Stonington history occurred in August 1814, when outgunned townspeople repelled an attack by five British warships under the command of Commodore Thomas Hardy during the War of 1812.

The town grew into a thriving port known for shipbuilding, sealing, and whaling. John M. Niles provided a snapshot of Stonington in 1819 in his volume *A Gazetteer of the States of Connecticut and Rhode Island.*

> *There are 1100 tons of shipping owned in this town, which are employed either in the business of fishing, or in the coasting and West India trade, and which furnish employment to a portion of the inhabitants. The maritime situation and interests of the town have given a direction to the pursuits and habits of its citizens; and Stonington has become conspicuous as a nursery of seamen, distinguished for their enterprise, perseverance and courage.*

Niles also reported that the town had 10 to 15 vessels engaged in fishing and a number engaged in coastal trade. The first Stonington sealing ship, the brig *Frederick*, sailed to Antarctic grounds in 1818. Captain Nathaniel B. Palmer of the sealing sloop *Hero* is credited with discovering the Antarctic continent two years later. Between the 1820s and the 1850s Stonington also had a number of vessels engaged in whaling.

With all this activity it's no surprise that in May of 1822, Congress appropriated $3,500 for a lighthouse at the east side of the entrance to the harbor. The new light would guide vessels passing through Fisher's Island Sound as well as those headed for the harbor in Stonington. The lighthouse was built the following year by contractor Benjamin Chase of Newport at a cost of $2,916.57, and it was first lit in 1824.

A 30-foot cylindrical stone tower was erected and the lantern was fitted with a system of 10 whale oil lamps with 13-inch parabolic reflectors. A fixed white light was exhibited from 47 feet above sea level. The first keeper, William Potter, lived in a stone dwelling built near the lighthouse and was paid a salary of $300 per year.

Stonington's lighthouse keepers occupied a special place in local society. "I often think of the keeper's eye in the tower," says Louise Pittaway, curator of the Old Lighthouse Museum. "He might well be the first to spot a long overdue whaler or trader who had been gone long enough to cause worry all around. When a vessel left harbor, it wasn't unusual for them to be gone from two to three years or longer. Often there was no word of their welfare until their vessel once again appeared on the horizon."

An 1838 report by Lt. George M. Bache of the U.S. Navy gave the lighthouse and keeper high marks but pointed out the severe erosion problem at the location:

> *The buildings of this establishment are . . . now in good order, the wooden stairway of the tower having been lately renewed.*
>
> *The lantern contains ten lamps with parabolic reflectors disposed around two horizontal iron tables. . . . The reflectors are 13 inches in diameter, and average in weight two pounds two ounces each. The whole apparatus is in good order, with the exception of the silver being much worn from the upper portion of the concave surfaces of the reflectors.*
>
> *The point of land on which the buildings stand is much exposed to the action of the waters during heavy south and southwesterly gales. High-water mark now lies within 45 feet of the tower, and the earth has been washed away to within 30 feet of the base. According to the account of the light-keeper, 22 feet of the bank has been carried away from the extremity of the point since the year 1823, and the same action has been going on, though in a less degree, to the eastward and westward of the dwelling. It will be advisable to protect these buildings from the encroachment of the sea, by constructing a wall.*

It was eventually decided that the cost of constructing a wall around the buildings would be at least equal to the cost of building

Stonington Harbor Lighthouse's granite spiral stairway. *Photo by the author.*

new ones. A wall also would not have been a permanent solution and probably would have protected the station for only a few years. The station was instead rebuilt farther north on the point, largely using the stones and materials from the earlier buildings.

The work was performed in September 1840 by John Bishop of New London. The rebuilding cost $4,914 in all, including $1,906 for a new cylindrical lantern and lighting equipment consisting of eight lamps and 16-inch reflectors. The new light was exhibited from 62 feet above sea level.

The 35-foot octagonal stone tower, about 10 feet in diameter, is built onto the front of the one-and-one-half-story dwelling. A spiral stairway of granite blocks leads to the lantern room. In the lighthouse's active days, the entire exterior was painted white or whitewashed.

William Potter died in 1842 and was replaced as keeper by Patty Potter, his wife. The Potters had four children, two of whom died before William became keeper. Their two other daughters probably helped their mother with the work of lighthouse keeping, but both of them had died by the time Patty retired in 1854.

An inspector's tour in 1848 produced a harsh report that called the building "the most filthy house" the inspector had ever visited. Maybe Patty just had an off week or perhaps her housekeeping improved, because an inspection two years later produced much more favorable results:

> *This building—for there is but one, the light being on the roof or on the tower connected with the house—we found in good order, except*

a little leaky. Lantern and lighting apparatus we found, as usual, in a neglected state. We put on a full set of iron burners.

Patty Potter retired at the age of 71 and died at 86.

The old system of lamps and reflectors was replaced by a sixth-order Fresnel lens in 1856. The Lighthouse Board reported in 1868 and 1869 that the station was in good condition and needed no repairs, but things apparently deteriorated quickly because the 1873 annual report stated, "Very extensive repairs are needed." Four years later it was reported, "This station has been greatly improved during the year by the erection of a substantial stone wall along its whole front, and by the grading of the light-house grounds."

The 1888 Annual Report of the Lighthouse Board signaled the end of the lighthouse's active years:

In consequence of the completion of the breakwater at the entrance of this harbor, the present light has ceased to be of any practical use as an aid to navigation. For some time past the Stonington and Providence Steam-boat Company has maintained, at its own expense, a private light and fog-signal on the eastern end of this breakwater. The Board therefore came to the conclusion that a

Stonington Breakwater Light, from an early 1900s postcard. *Courtesy of Michel Forand.*

public light and fog-signal should be established here, and it estimated the cost for doing this at $8,000. . . . When this is done the present light will be discontinued.

A 25-foot conical cast-iron tower on the breakwater was completed and put into operation along with a fog bell on November 1, 1889. On the same day the old lighthouse went dark. Benjamin Pendleton, a former whaler and sealer who had been keeper at the old lighthouse since 1872, became the first keeper of the breakwater light. A small shack was provided on the breakwater, but Pendleton spent most of his time living in the 1840 stone lighthouse.

One of the breakwater light's keepers was George W. Beckwith, a Civil War veteran and a ship steward for many years. The keeper for several years beginning in 1898 was Joseph J. Fuller, a former whaling captain from New London. In his whaling days Fuller was once shipwrecked in the Antarctic, where he remained for a year before being rescued. He also served under Adm. David Farragut during the Civil War both in Mobile Bay and on the Mississippi.

Even though keepers were still living there, the 1840 lighthouse was allowed to deteriorate. A letter dated December 7, 1901, from the Secretary of the Treasury to the Speaker of the House of Representatives pleaded for the construction of a new dwelling:

A recent inspection of the Stonington Breakwater, Connecticut, light-station has shown that its keeper's dwelling is in a condition so unhealthful as to menace the lives of its occupants, there having been more or less sickness in every family residing therein during the past twenty years. The house is very old, no work has been done on it for a long time, it is past economical repair, and is in such a condition as to make it almost uninhabitable.

The Lighthouse Board asked for $6,000 for a new dwelling, but despite the urgency of the situation nothing was done until 1908, when the funds were appropriated and a new dwelling was built next to the old lighthouse. That house still stands, though it is greatly changed and enlarged. The breakwater lighthouse was dismantled in 1926 and replaced by an automated light on a skeleton tower.

In 1925 the old lighthouse was offered for public sale, and the only bidder was Eugene Atwood on behalf of the Stonington Historical and Genealogical Society. That organization was soon incorporated as the Stonington Historical Society. A committee was formed to oversee the restoration of the lighthouse, and the interior was remodeled to make way for a museum. The biggest change in the lighthouse's exterior appearance was the addition of diamond-paned windows in the front. A fireplace and second chimney were apparently added at about the same time.

The society soon began to house its collection of historic artifacts in the building. It is appropriate that this seafaring town should have a museum in a lighthouse, and Stonington's proud legacy is well represented in the Old Lighthouse Museum. The building itself and the eclectic collection have been beautifully maintained over the years by staff and volunteers.

The Stonington Historical Society suffered a setback when the great hurricane of September 21, 1938, walloped New England's south-facing coast. Part of the roof was blown off, a terrace was destroyed, and a great deal of the east shoreline was washed away. The terrace, which had been used as a tearoom in summer, was not rebuilt. Repairs were gradually made to the building and grounds.

Louise Pittaway, curator of the museum since the 1980s, grew up in upstate New York far from water, "other than the small creek at the bottom of the hill." After coming to Stonington, Pittaway made it part of her mission to stretch the season and hours of public access at the lighthouse, to the point that the museum is now open from 10:00 a.m. to 5:00 p.m. from May to November, seven days a week in the peak months and by appointment in the off-season.

There's no other lighthouse on the Connecticut coast that's open as often. "It pleases me that our lighthouse has been a leader in welcoming visitors inside and allowing them access to the tower," Pittaway says, "unlike so many that can only be viewed from the grounds. I think townspeople are proud of our lighthouse and its fine museum, and think of it as an important local point of interest."

"There are six rooms to enjoy," says Pittaway, with "exhibits that offer a diverse and surprising quality—everything from nautical tools and scrimshaw, China trade items, pre-1835 Stonington pottery and other early pieces, ice harvesting tools and photos, a room of children's exhibits and large doll house, Battle of Stonington and other military items, and a changing feature exhibit each season."

Also upstairs is a fourth-order Fresnel lens, nicely exhibited in a protective case donated by the New England Lighthouse Lovers (NELL). Visitors get to climb the stairs into the lantern room, and the panoramic view encompasses parts of three states: Rhode Island, Connecticut, and New York.

In 2003 a four-foot-square glass panel was added in the museum floor, affording visitors a look at a large, round stone cistern as they approach the stairs to the upstairs exhibits. This cistern once collected rainwater from the roof for the keepers and their families, the only source of freshwater in the light's active years. A second glass-covered opening in the floor reveals a well, but "the water is brackish—thus the need for the cistern," Pittaway explains.

One of the lighthouse's distinctive features is the arrow weathervane atop the lantern. It isn't clear when it was first installed. "It appears in all photos," says Pittaway, "but who knows about earlier?" In 2003 the weathervane, which had been stuck in a north-south position, was taken apart. After the addition of a new bearing and lubrication, it now again does its job.

When asked why people should visit Stonington's Old Lighthouse Museum, Pittaway says, "People of all ages seem to find something they like among the exhibits, and they enjoy the chance to climb the tower. My hope is that every visitor might feel their visit has taught them something new."

But there's also that intangible "something" about lighthouses. "I can't imagine anyone not loving lighthouses," she says. "They seem to symbolize something almost spiritual. How comforting it must have been to the sailor in rough seas as they provided a path of light in the darkness, doing their best to keep him from treacherous rocks. And for myself, now that I have the smell of the sea in my nose, I can't imagine living anywhere else."

To reach the Old Lighthouse Museum, take Exit 91 off I-95. Turn south on Route 234 (Pequot Trail) and go 0.4 mile to North Main Street. Turn left on North Main Street and continue 1.5 miles to a light at the intersection with U.S. Route 1. Cross Route 1 and continue straight to a stop sign. Turn left and then take the next right over a viaduct (railroad bridge) onto Water Street. Follow Water Street through Stonington Village to the end. Park at the end of the point and walk back to the lighthouse.

To find out more about the Stonington Historical Society and the Old Lighthouse Museum, you can call (860) 535-1440, or visit their Web site at www.stoningtonhistory.org.

Above: The 1910 light and fog bell tower built on New Haven's Long Wharf. *Courtesy of Bob Shanley.*

Below: Essex Reef Light, also known as Hayden's Point Light, from an old postcard. *From the author's collection.*

Miscellaneous Lights and Lightships

New Haven Long Wharf Light

The first light established on New Haven's Long Wharf in 1854 was a simple iron post light. A new iron tower with a fixed red light 45 feet above the water was installed along with a fog bell in 1900. There was never a keeper's house near the wharf, and since keepers didn't live on-site, vandalism caused many problems over the years. In July 1912 a fire was set that did a tremendous amount of damage to nearby storage buildings.

Thomas F. Wilson, a well-known character on New Haven's waterfront, was keeper of this light for about 15 years. He had worked in a chandlery on Long Wharf and was said to know all the local captains and to have an encyclopedic knowledge of all things nautical. He would sail his yawl around the harbor, buying up spare equipment from tugs and other vessels that he would later resell. Locals knew the light simply as "Tom's Light."

In late September 1910 the captain of a passing steamer noticed that the light at Long Wharf was dark. An investigation revealed that 58-year-old Keeper Tom Wilson had died on a landing inside the tower of a hemorrhage just as he was about to light the beacon for the night.

A skeletal tower at this location with an automated flashing green light remains an active aid to navigation.

Essex Reef Light and Chester Rock Light

Two small (21-foot) hexagonal wooden towers were built on the Connecticut River in 1889 to aid navigation toward Hartford. Essex Reef Light, also known as Hayden's Point Light, was near the town of Essex, and Chester Rock Light was farther north, near Chester. Both had sixth-order lenses and neither had resident keepers. They were maintained by attendants who lived nearby. Both were inactive by 1919 and were demolished.

Mystic Seaport Lighthouse

This was never an official aid to navigation, but it does have a fourth-order Fresnel lens that was loaned by the Coast Guard. The small wooden lighthouse on the grounds of the popular Mystic Seaport maritime museum complex is a near-replica of the 1901 Brant Point Light on Nantucket.

Bartlett Reef Lightship

Dangerous Bartlett Reef is located off Waterford, Connecticut. A lightship was first stationed here, about three and a half miles southwest of New London Harbor Light, in 1835. The first small wooden vessel was replaced by a larger one in 1848. This 150-ton vessel, the LV-17, had been built nearby in Stonington. The 79-foot LV-13 served at the station from 1867 to 1933, when it was discontinued. Today the reef is marked by a skeleton tower with an automatic flashing white light.

Stratford Shoal Lightship

See Chapter 10.

Cornfield Point Lightship

In 1856 a 91-foot lightship with a single lantern was stationed offshore from the mouth of the Connecticut River near Old Saybrook, south of the center of Long Sand Shoal. It was more than three miles from Lynde Point Lighthouse. Several vessels were stationed here over the years, and there were a number of accidents involving other vessels.

The LV-13 (Bartlett Reef Lightship). *From the collection of Edward Rowe Snow, courtesy of Dorothy Bicknell.*

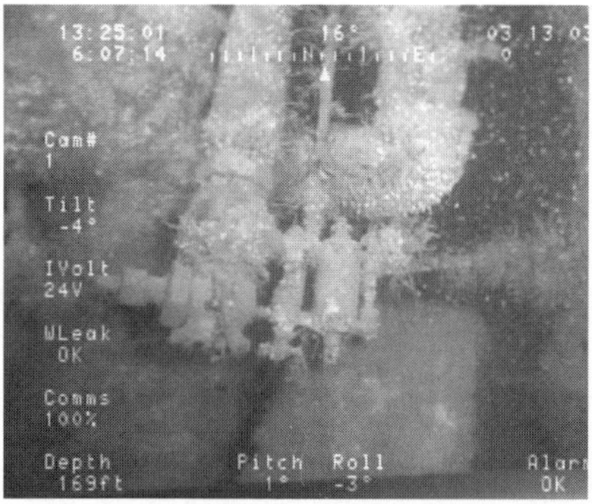

Engine and generator on the lightship LV-51, as seen via NOAA's National Undersea Research Center remotely operated vehicle, the P3S2. *Courtesy of Ivar G. Babb, Director, National Undersea Research Center for the North Atlantic and Great Lakes, University of Connecticut.*

LV-51 was a steel-hulled lightship built by F. W. Wheeler and Company in West Bay City, Michigan, in 1892. It was the first lightship in the world to use electric lights as aids to navigation, and the first to have an engine for propulsion. The LV-51 served at the Cornfield Point station until 1894. After serving some years at the Sandy Hook lightship station, it became a relief lightship.

On April 19, 1919, the LV-51 was back at the Cornfield Point station when it was rammed by a Standard Oil barge being towed by a tugboat. The lightship sank in eight minutes but the entire crew was able to escape to a lifeboat. The vessel and its contents were a total loss. In 2003 the National Oceanic and Atmospheric Administration's National Undersea Research Center at the University of Connecticut validated the identity of the wreck lying in 180 feet of water on the bottom of Long Island Sound. It was subsequently designated an underwater State Archaeological Preserve.

The Cornfield Point station was discontinued in 1957.

Ram Island Reef Lightship

This station was established in 1886 south of Mystic. The first vessel stationed here, the 85-foot LV-19, had been in service since 1845. It was driven from its station at Ram Island Reef several times by drifting ice.

The 94-foot LV-23, formerly at the Cornfield Point station, replaced the LV-19 in 1894. The old LV-19 was then used by the navy for target practice. Crewmen from the LV-23 were responsible for saving the lives of at least five people in the vicinity. The station was discontinued in 1925.

SELECTED BIBLIOGRAPHY

More extensive bibliographies for each of the lighthouses in this book can be found on the author's Web site at www.lighthouse.cc.

General Sources

Adamson, Hans Christian. *Keepers of the Lights.* New York: Greenberg, 1955.

Annual Reports of the Lighthouse Board. Clipping files, Records Group 26, National Archives, Washington, DC.

Bachand, Robert G. *Northeast Lights: Lighthouses and Lightships, Rhode Island to Cape May, New Jersey.* Norwalk, CT: Sea Sports Publications, 1989.

Bridgeport (Conn.) Public Library. Historical Collections, miscellaneous clippings.

Brilvitch, Charles. *Walking through History: The Seaports of Black Rock and Southport.* Fairfield, CT: Fairfield Historical Society, 1977.

Cahill, Robert Ellis. *Lighthouse Mysteries of the North Atlantic.* Salem, MA: Salt Box, 1998.

Caulkins, Frances Manwaring. *History of New London, Connecticut.* New London, CT: Frances M. Caulkins, 1852.

Citro, Joseph A. *Passing Strange: True Tales of New England Hauntings and Horrors.* Boston: Houghton Mifflin, 1996.

Clifford, Mary Louise, and J. Candace Clifford. *Women Who Kept the Lights: An Illustrated History of Female Lighthouse Keepers.* Williamsburg, VA: Cypress Communications, 1993.

Connecticut: A Guide to Its Roads, Lore, and People. WPA Writers Program, 1938.

Connecticut Historical Commission. National Register of Historic Places registration forms.

Danenberg, Elsie Nicholas. *The Story of Bridgeport.* Bridgeport, CT: Bridgeport Centennial, 1936.

Delaney, Edmund T. *The Connecticut Shore.* New York: Weathervane Books, 1969.

De Wire, Elinor. *Guardians of the Lights: The Men and Women of the U.S. Lighthouse Service.* Sarasota, FL: Pineapple Press, 1995.

———. *Sentries along the Shore.* Gales Ferry, CT: Sentinel Publications, 1997.

Gleason, Sarah C. *Kindly Lights: A History of the Lighthouses of Southern New England.* Boston: Beacon Press, 1991.

Hamilton, Harlan. *Lights and Legends: A Historical Guide to Lighthouses of Long Island Sound, Fishers Island Sound, and Block Island Sound.* Stamford, CT: Wescott Cove Publishing Company, 1987.

Hayward, John. *New England Gazetteer.* Boston: John Hayward, 1839.

Hayward, Marjorie F. *The East Side of New Haven Harbor.* New Haven: New Haven Colony Historical Society, 1938.

Historic Sites Survey, Inventory, and Analysis of Aids to Navigation in the State of Connecticut. West Chester, PA: John Milner Associates, Inc., May 1986.

Holland, Francis Ross, Jr. *America's Lighthouses: An Illustrated History.* Brattleboro, VT: Stephen Greene Press, 1972. Reprint, New York: Dover, 1988.

Justinius, Ivan O. *History of Black Rock.* Bridgeport, CT: Antoniak Printing Service, 1955.

Knapp, Lewis G. *In Pursuit of Paradise: History of the Town of Stratford, Connecticut.* Stratford Historical Society, 1989.

———. *Stratford and the Sea.* Charleston, SC: Arcadia Publishing, 2002.
Kochel, Kenneth G. *America's Atlantic Coast Lighthouses: A Traveler's Guide.* Rev. ed. Wells, ME: Lighthouse Digest, 2000.
Letter from the Secretary of the Treasury transmitting the report of the general superintendent of the light-house establishment, Dec. 20, 1850. House of Representatives, 31st Congress, 2d session, Doc. No. 14.
Lighthouse clippings files at U.S. Coast Guard Historian's Office, Washington, DC.
Lighthouse Directory. www.unc.edu/~rowlett/lighthouse/.
Lighthouse Explorer Database. www.lighthousedigest.com/database/searchdatabase.cfm.
Marcus, Jon. *Lighthouses of New England.* Stillwater, MN: Voyageur Press, 2001.
Marshall, Benjamin Tinkham. *A Modern History of New London County, Connecticut.* New York: Lewis Historical Publishing, 1922.
Memorials, Reports and Statistics Concerning Improvement of New Haven Harbor. New Haven: Tuttle, Morehouse & Taylor, 1879.
Mills, Robert. *The American Pharos, or Light-House Guide.* Washington, DC: Thompson & Homans, 1832.
Mueller, Robert G. *Long Island's Lighthouses, Past and Present.* Interlaken, NY: Heart of the Lakes Publishing, 2004.
National Park Service. *Inventory of Historic Light Stations.* Washington, DC: GPO, 1994.
New Haven Colony Historical Society. Miscellaneous clippings.
Noank: Celebrating a Maritime Heritage. Noank, CT: Noank Historical Society, 2002.
Noble, Dennis L. *Lighthouses & Keepers.* Annapolis, MD: Naval Institute Press, 1997.
Orcutt, Samuel. *A History of the Old Town of Stratford and the City of Bridgeport, Connecticut.* 2 vols. Fairfield County Historical Society, 1886.
Palmer, Henry Robinson. *Stonington by the Sea.* Stonington, CT: Palmer Press, 1957.
Putnam, George R. *Lighthouses and Lightships of the United States.* Boston: Houghton Mifflin, 1933.
Rathbun, Benjamin F. *Capsule Histories of Some Local Islands and Lighthouses in the Eastern Part of Long Island Sound.* Niantic, CT: Presley Printing, 1996.
Ray, Deborah W., and Gloria P. Stewart. *Norwalk, Being an Historical Account of That Connecticut Town.* Canaan, NH: Phoenix Press, 1979.
Rhein, Michael J. *Anatomy of the Lighthouse.* New York: Barnes and Noble Books, 2000.
Roberts, Bruce, and Ray Jones. *New England Lighthouses: Bay of Fundy to Long Island Sound.* Old Saybrook, CT: Globe Pequot Press, 1996.
Sheffield—From Legend to Lighthouse. Greenwich, CT: Damselfly Design, 1992.
Snow, Edward Rowe. *Famous Lighthouses of America.* New York: Dodd, Mead & Company, 1955.
Stark, Charles R. *Groton, Conn. 1705–1905.* Stonington, CT: The Palmer Press, 1922.
Steitz, George C. *Haunted Lighthouses and How to Find Them.* Sarasota, FL: Pineapple Press, 2002.
Stevenson, D. Alan. *The World's Lighthouses from Ancient Times to 1820.* London: Oxford University Press, 1959. Reprint, Mineola, NY: Dover, 2002.
Stratford (Conn.) Historical Society. Clippings file, miscellaneous clippings.
U.S. Coast Guard District One Aids to Navigation Office, Boston, MA. Aids to navigation files.
Wiencek, Henry. *The Smithsonian Guide to Historic America: Southern New England.* New York: Stewart, Tabori, and Cheng, 1989.
Wilcoxson, William Howard. *History of Stratford, Connecticut, 1639–1969.* Stratford, CT: Stratford Tercentenary Commission, 1969.
Williams, Dick. *The Historic Norwalk Islands.* Darien, CT: Pictorial Associates, 1978.

Chapter 1, Great Captain Island Light

Berger, Meyer. "Lighthouse Crew Welcomes Spring." *New York Times*, Mar. 15, 1949.
Collins, Libby. "Anything Goes." *The Greenwich Review*, Mar. 1976.
Cowles, Gregory. "No Man Is an Island (but Great Captain's Caretaker Otto Lauersdorf Comes Pretty Close)." *Greenwich Time*, Aug. 20, 2000.
Greenwich Historical Society Newsletter. "Great Captain's Light," July 1987.
Greenwich Social Review. "The Ups and Downs of Great Captain's Island," June 1965.
Hewitt, Arthur. "Signals of the Sea." *Outlook*, Nov. 1904.
Layton, Arthur. "Coast Guard Crew Preparing to Abandon Lonesome Vigil on Great Captain Island." *Greenwich Time*, Oct. 31, 1968.
Linskey, Annie. "Lighting the Way to Remembrance." *Greenwich Time*, Sept. 8, 2003.
New York Herald. "Siren Is Breaking Up Happy Homes," June 19, 1905.
New York Times. "Lighthouse Case Settled," Aug. 4, 1907.
Stevens, John W. "Greenwich Sees the Ghost of 1656." *New York Times*, Aug. 1, 1956.
Strong, Roger W. "Keepers of the Greenwich Isles." *New York Times*, July 3, 1977.

Chapter 2, Stamford Harbor Light

Ada Evening News (Oklahoma). "Heroine Passes Night of Terror," May 7, 1908.
Anderson, David. "Stamford Light, Scene of Murder and Romance, Faces Destruction." *New York Times*, June 16, 1953.
Bridgeport Telegram. "Double Fatality—Inquest Unneeded," Jan. 24, 1927.
Carella, Angela. "Lighthouse Is Beacon of History." *Stamford Advocate*, Sept. 30, 1991.
Cavanaugh, Jack. "A Lighthouse and a Cleanup on the Sound." *New York Times*, Sept. 28, 1997.
"Christmas Cheer in a Lighthouse," Dec. 17, 1908. Newspaper unknown. From clippings file, Stamford Historical Society, Stamford, CT.
Crabill, Steven. "Flash: Lighthouse Goes for $230,000." *Stamford Advocate*, Dec. 15, 1984.
———. "Spring Cleaning Is No Lightweight Chore for Lighthouse Owner." *Stamford Advocate*, June 10, 1985.
Davenport, Peter. "Area's Oldest Lighthouse Is a Survivor." *Stamford Advocate*, July 14, 2004.
Lighthouse Service Bulletin, July 1, 1929.
Marin, Tim. "Summer Home in a Lighthouse." *Stamford Advocate*, June 25, 1967.
New York Times. "Group Buys Lighthouse Without Knowing Why," Feb. 9, 1968.
———. "L. I. Sound May Lose Famed Lighthouse," June 16, 1949.
———. "Would-Be Buyers Visit Lighthouse," Jan. 26, 1955.
Nova, Susan. "A Beacon Beckons." *Greenwich Time*, June 6, 1997.
Russell, Don. "Lighthouse History a Bit Less Than Shining." *Stamford Advocate*, Aug. 19, 1998.
Stamford Advocate. "Believe Stamford Light Keeper Lost in Sound as Capsized Boat Is Found," Aug. 15, 1931.
———. "Body of R. E. Bliven, Stamford Light Keeper, Found in Sound, Saturday," Aug. 16, 1931.
———. "Coast Guard Enlightens Those Wanting to Buy Old Lighthouse," July 7, 1967.
———. "For Sale: One Lighthouse," Nov. 12, 1953.
———. "Harbor Lighthouse Transferred Back to Federal Control," Sept. 8, 1966.
———. "Stamford Lighthouse Closing; New Harbor Signals Announced," May 22, 1953.
———. "Trio Submits Highest Bid for Stamford Lighthouse," Aug. 1, 1967.
Sunday News. "Old Stamford Light to Blink Awhile," June 14, 1953.

Chapter 3, Green's Ledge Light
Harrison, Timothy. "A Mystery from the Past." *Lighthouse Digest*, Mar. 2002.
New York Times. "Starved in Lighthouse, Dies," Feb. 24, 1911.
Norwalk Hour. "Kiarskon Held for Forgery," Mar. 12, 1910.
———. "Light Man's Trying Time," Mar. 3, 1910.
———. "Lighthouse Man Found," Mar. 11, 1910.
Washington Post, "Famine in a Lighthouse," Mar. 17, 1912.
———. "Hero Kept Beacon Lit," Mar. 13, 1910.
———. "A True Spartan," Mar. 14, 1910.

Chapter 4, Sheffield Island Light
Adams, Virginia Queen. *History of Sheffield Island, Norwalk, Connecticut.* Stamford, CT, 1968.
Aport, Helm. "Best Summer of My Life—Andy Siegel." *Norwalk Hour*, Sept. 14, 1988.
Bodach, Jill. "New Lighthouse Keeper Ready." *Norwalk Hour*, June 10, 2003.
Coneybear, John F. "Ownership of Sheffield Light Passes to Seaport Association."
Connolly, Kathy, and Paul Connolly. "The Two Norwalks." *Offshore*, Sept. 1988.
Guevin, Laura. "On Watch at the Lighthouse." *Norwalk Hour*, May 13, 1995.
Hazell, Naedine Joy. "Toast of the Coast: Norwalk Islands Have an Intriguing History." *Hartford Courant*, July 6, 1997.
Norwalk Gazette, July 29, 1818; Aug. 15, 1826; Dec. 21, 1842; Jan. 4, 1843; Feb. 5, 1845; July 30, 1845; Aug. 17, 1849; Aug. 2, 1870.
Norwalk Hour, Dec. 31, 1986.
The Seaport Sun, newsletter of the Norwalk Seaport Association. Various issues, 1997–2004.
Stamford Advocate. "Job of Lighthouse Keeper at Sheffield Island Has Few Modern Perks to Offer," May 15, 2003.
von Zielbauer, Paul. "A Lighthouse Keeper Loves the Life, Even in the Dark." *New York Times*, July 16, 2003.

Chapter 5, Peck's Ledge Light
Naugatuck Daily News, Dec. 3, 1901.
Norwalk Hour, Feb. 10, 1933.
———. "Light at Peck's Ledge Shines Out," July 11, 1906.
———. "New Light at Peck's Ledge," May 26, 1905.
———. "Steam Canaler 'Austin' Sank at Norwalk Light Monday Night; Four on Board Barely Escaping," Dec. 7, 1921.

Chapter 6, Penfield Reef Light
Baldor, Lolita C. "Memories Haunt Penfield Lighthouse." *Fairfield Citizen-News*, July 22, 1983.
Barrow, F. A. "Wanderings in and about Bridgeport." *Bridgeport Sunday Post*, May 14, 1922. From clippings file in Bridgeport Public Library, Historical Collections.
Bridgeport Post, "Penfield Lighthouse to Go Automatic on Saturday," Sept. 2, 1971.
———. "William Hardwick Dies in 78th Year," Nov. 24, 1954.
———. "Yes, Penfield Light Erratic, Coast Guard Vessel Reports," Mar. 16, 1972.
"Cows Browsed on Reef Years Ago, Keeper Believes." Newspaper unknown, ca. 1920s. From clippings file in Bridgeport Public Library, Historical Collections.
DeBlois, Frank. "Tales of a Not-So-Ancient Connecticut Mariner." *Bridgeport Post*, Mar. 2, 1941.
D'Entremont, Jeremy. "Connecticut's Penfield Reef Light: No Longer Ghostly." *Lighthouse Digest*, Oct. 2002.

Fairfield Town Crier. "96-Year-Old Lighthouse Wins Demolition Stay," Jan. 17, 1970.
"Lighthouse Keepers Bow to Automation Takeover." Newspaper unknown, Dec. 3, 1971. From clippings file in Bridgeport Public Library, Historical Collections.
Lighthouse Service Bulletin, Vol. III, No. 62, Feb. 1, 1929, p. 278.
———. Vol. IV, No. 11, Nov. 1, 1930, p. 46.
Morris, Major H. C. "Sunken Chimes Are Said to Still Ring Warning." *Bridgeport Post,* n.d. From clippings file in Bridgeport Public Library, Historical Collections.
New York Times. "A Lighthouse Keeper Adrift," Jan. 30, 1888.
Petzolt, Harold. "Lessons My Father Told Me." *Lighthouse Digest,* Aug. 1995.
"Vow Visits of Ghostly Being Have Followed Drowning of Former Keeper." From clippings file in Bridgeport Public Library, Historical Collections.

Chapter 7, Black Rock Harbor Light

Bridgeport Daily Standard, Mar. 25, 1878.
Bridgeport News. "Efforts Begin to Restore Lighthouse in Black Rock Harbor," Jan. 11, 1996.
———. "On the Evening of Gala Event, Lighthouse Is Mysteriously Lit," Apr. 25, 1996.
Bridgeport Post. "Board Tries to Save Lighthouse," Jan. 22, 1980.
———. "City Is Given Deed to Fayerweather," July 18, 1934.
Clark, James G. "Fund-Raising Effort Is a Shining Success." *Connecticut Post,* Aug. 17, 1997.
———. "Light Blight." *Connecticut Post,* Apr. 23, 1998.
———. "With Work, Lighthouse Shines." *Connecticut Post,* Nov. 14, 1998.
Columbian Centinel. "Interesting to Mariners," Dec. 8, 1808.
———. Dec. 14, 1808.
Connecticut Post, "A Colorful History Inhabits Long-Neglected Lighthouse." Letter from Faith Clark Van Louvender, July 30, 1996.
D'Entremont, Jeremy. "Fayerweather Island Light Brought Back to Life." *Lighthouse Digest,* July 2000.
Fairfield Citizen News. "Lighthouse Keeper Kate," Jan. 16, 1996.
Fitzsimmons, Kim. "Keepers of the Light." *Connecticut Post,* Apr. 3, 1994.
Johnson, Reginald. "Fayerweather Island: From Ruin to Recovery." *Connecticut Post,* Oct. 19, 2003.
Matthews, Cara. "A Light Returns to New Glory: Citizen Effort Helps Restore Fayerweather." *Connecticut Post,* Apr. 27, 2000.
New York Sunday World. "A Lifetime in a Lighthouse," 1889 [exact date unknown]. From clippings file in Bridgeport Public Library, Historical Collections.
Szivos, Frank. "Shining a Light on Black Rock." *Republican-American (CT),* Oct. 3, 1994.
Witkowski, Mary. "Black Rock Was Home to Lighthouse Keepers." *Bridgeport News,* Oct. 29, 1998.

Chapter 8, Bridgeport Harbor Light

Bridgeport Post. "Air of Romance Surrounding Lighthouse Exerts Fascination for Casual Visitor," Aug. 30, 1925.
———. "How Bridgeport Lighthouse Evolved from Spile Driven in Channel by Capt. McNeil," Nov. 26, 1922.
———. "Lighthouse Leveled by Fire While Being Dismantled," Dec. 20, 1953.
———. "Uncle Sam Modernizes 64-Year-Old Lighthouse Here," July 31, 1935.
Bridgeport Standard. "One of the Beacon Lights." June 24, 1887. From clippings file in Bridgeport Public Library, Historical Collections.

Bridgeport Telegram. "Find Two Bodies of Lighter's Crew," Dec. 22, 1920.
———. "Steam Lighter on Which Three Lost Lives Is Located," May 21, 1921.
Lockwood, Alma R. "Century-Old Bridgeport Lighthouse to Be Replaced by Automatic Signals." *Bridgeport Post,* Aug. 29, 1953.
New York Times. "Century-Old Lighthouse to Die by Fire," Aug. 25, 1953.
———. "A Lighthouse Damaged by Ice," Feb. 9, 1886.
Tabor, Deva. "Woman Braves Storm to Flash Warning Signals to Vessels Being Piloted Toward Safety in Harbor." Newspaper unknown, Oct. 26, 1913. From clippings file in Bridgeport Public Library, Historical Collections.
Von Gal, Geraldine. "Light Housekeeper Looks Forward to Time When She May Be Lighthouse Keeper." Newspaper unknown, Jan. 23, 1930. From clippings file in Bridgeport Public Library, Historical Collections.
Whelan, Ann. "All 'At Sea' but Happy Is the Lighthouse Boy." *Bridgeport Sunday Post,* May 30, 1937.

Chapter 9, Tongue Point Light

Bridgeport Daily Standard. "A New Lighthouse," Jan. 16, 1891.
Bridgeport Post. "Boaters in Area Protest; Harbor Light Will Stay," Sept. 8, 1967.
———. "Coast Guard May Discontinue Tongue Point Light, Fog Signal," Aug. 9, 1967.
Tabor, Deva. "Woman Braves Storm to Flash Warning Signals to Vessels Being Piloted Toward Safety in Harbor." Newspaper unknown, Oct. 26, 1913. From clippings file in Bridgeport Public Library, Historical Collections.

Chapter 10, Stratford Shoal Light

Boston Globe. "Lighthouse Men Lauded for Saugatuck Rescue," Feb. 26, 1933.
Bridgeport Post. "Grounded Tanker Has Lighthouse for Company," May 17, 1955.
———. "Jet Is Crippled, Pilot Rescued," June 24, 1955.
———. "Middleground Light Goes Fully Automatic on July 11," June 4, 1979.
———. "Tanker Strikes Reef at Middleground Light," May 6, 1955.
Bridgeport Telegram. "Adrift on Sound for 20 Hours When Boat's Propeller Jams," Jan. 21, 1920.
———. "Boat Damaged by Ice," Feb. 1, 1955.
Charleston Daily Mail. "Ten Adrift at Sea in Storm Rescued," Feb. 11, 1933.
Geller, Herbert F. "A Beacon to Mariners for 133 Years, Middleground Light Now Automated." *Bridgeport Sunday Post,* Mar. 27, 1977.
Iowa Citizen. "Struggle of a Week," Aug. 11, 1905.
Ironwood (MI) Daily Globe. "Ten Saved from Crippled Boat," Feb. 11, 1933.
Lighthouse Service Bulletin. Vol. IV, No. 8, Aug. 1, 1930, p. 34.
New York Times. "A Lighthouse Keeper Missing," Mar. 18, 1887.
Norwalk Hour. "Lighthouse Hero Lives in Norwalk." Feb. 11, 1933.
"One of the Beacon Lights." Newspaper unknown, 1887 [exact date unknown]. From clippings file in Bridgeport Public Library, Historical Collections.
Sandusky Star Journal. "Maniac—Tried to Destroy Stratford Shoals Light," Aug. 12, 1905.
Washington Post. "How Crafty Maniacs Have Attacked Persons out of Reach of Help," Sept. 29, 1907.

Chapter 11, Stratford Point Light

Bridgeport Post. "Personnel Leave CG Lighthouse," May 30, 1978.
———. "Stratford Light Keeper to Retire after 38 Years; History of Original Beacon Built a Century Ago," July 7, 1918.
"A Girl Heroine." Newspaper and date unknown. From clippings file, Stratford Historical Society.

Kirtland, Alex. "New Look Will Be an Old One for Lighthouse." *Bridgeport Post*, Apr. 12, 1990.
Neville, Jean. "Lighthouse Keeping Day and Night Job." Newspaper and date unknown. From clippings file, Stratford Historical Society.
New York Times. "Captain Judson Dead in Bridgeport," May 14, 1935.
Newark Daily Advocate. "A Big Sea Serpent," July 31, 1896.
———. "Lighthouse Keeper Sights a Submarine," July 22, 1916.
Nonnenmacher, P. T. "'Naked' Lighthouse Gets Cupola." *Bridgeport Post*, June 29, 1990.
Stratford News. "Beacon Shines Again at Historic Stratford Point," July 26, 1990.
Tabor, Ruth. "Lighthouse Guides Ships since 1882." *Stratford News*, Sept. 8, 1989.
———. "Stratford Point's First Lighthouse Built in 1821." *Stratford News*, Sept. 15, 1988.
———. "Stratford's Resident Keeper of the Light." *Stratford News*, Aug. 25, 1988.
Taylor, Mary Darlington. "When Stratford's Historic Light Was Dimmed—and Why." *Bridgeport Sunday Post*, Mar. 13, 1938.
"Theed Judson Retires," Newspaper unknown, 1921 [exact date unknown]. From clippings file, Stratford Historical Society.
Watt, Dee. "Lighthouse Lens to Remain at Boothe Park." *Stratford News*, Mar. 16,1989.
Watt, J. L. "Lighthouse Re-Dedicated." *Stratford News*, July 17, 1990.
Wentworth, Hugh. "Coast Guard Family Enjoys Lighthouse Life." *Stratford Star*, Sept. 26, 1990.

Chapter 12, Five Mile Point Light

American Mercury. "A Summer Retreat," June 28, 1810.
Beach, Randall. "New Haven Is Quite a Sight from the Top of the Harbor Light." *New Haven Register*, Oct. 23, 2002.
Boston Globe. "Connecticut Lighthouse Receives a Facelift from City Officials," May 11, 1986.
D'Entremont, Jeremy. "New Haven's Old Beacon Opened to the Public." *Lighthouse Digest*, Jan. 2003.
"Light Keeper Passes Away." Unidentified and undated clipping from the collection of the New Haven Colony Historical Society.
Matthews, Kenneth. "Lighthouse Life: 20 Years by Sea." *New Haven Journal-Courier*, Aug. 30, 1964.
New Haven Register. "Beach Opens at Lighthouse Point Park," May 29, 1955.
———. "Lighthouse Gets First Paint in 20 Years," May 25, 1949.
New York Times. "The Lightkeepers' Tales," Jan. 11, 1891.
———. "New Haven's Old Lighthouse," Aug. 1, 1890.

Chapter 13, Southwest Ledge Light

Letter from the Secretary of the Treasury in answer to a resolution of the House of Representatives, Mar. 20, 1872, relative to removing the lighthouse at New Haven Harbor to Southwest Ledge. 42d Congress, 2d session. Ex. Doc. No. 267, Apr. 18, 1872.
Lighthouse Digest. "Maintenance on Southwest Ledge Light," July 2001.
New Haven Register. "No Man There to Save Hero," Jan. 22, 1908.
New York Times. "Hero Cut His Throat," Jan. 23, 1908.

Chapter 14, Sperry Light

New Haven Register. "Along Memory Lane," Sept. 12, 1948.
———. July 16, 1933.

Chapter 15, Faulkner's Island Light

Boyle, Alix. "Restoring a Lighthouse Without Erasing Its History." *New York Times*, Aug. 31, 1997.

Bridgeport Telegram. "Lighthouse Keeper, Unconscious, Saved from Drift to Sea," Oct. 24, 1924.

Chapin, Vivian Jensen. "Faulkner's Island Sojourn." *Lighthouse Digest*, Feb. 2003.

Dale, Mabel. "Fire Devastates Faulkner's." *Guilford (CT) Shore Line Times*, Mar. 18, 1976.

Dee, Jane E. "The Light Brigade Team from New York Gets Charge Out of Restoration Project." *Hartford Courant*, Dec. 1, 1998.

———. "A Tale of Too Many Rabbits — Former Pets Breed Trouble for Tiny Island." *Hartford Courant*, Aug. 10, 1998.

D'Entremont, Jeremy. "Bicentennial Beacon Beams Brightly on Birthday." *Lighthouse Digest*, Nov. 2002.

———. "A 200th Birthday Present: Faulkner's Island Lighthouse Removed from Doomsday List." *Lighthouse Digest*, Jan. 2002.

Eastwood, Ted. "Three Men on a Rock." *New Haven Register*, Mar. 7, 1965.

Gardiner (ME) Home Journal. "Life in a Lighthouse: Captain Brooks' Long Service," May 16, 1888.

Hartford Daily Times. "A Lighthouse Keeper," July 7, 1881.

Helander, Joel E. *The Island Called Faulkner's*. Guilford, CT: Joel E. Helander, 1988.

Iacobellis, Margaret H. "From Doomsday List to Survivor's List." *Lighthouse Digest*, Jan. 1997.

Lowell Journal and Courier. "A Hero," Dec. 6, 1858.

New York Times. "Battles Ice Five Hours," Feb. 19, 1923.

Norton, Frederick Calvin. "Romantic Faulkner's Island." *Hartford Daily Courant*, Sept. 2, 1934.

The Octagon: Newsletter of the Faulkner's Light Brigade. Various issues, 1997–1999.

Stone, Clara J. *Genealogy of the Descendants of Jasper Griffing*. 1881.

Washington Post. "'Hero of 1858' Is Dead," Jan. 7, 1913.

Chapter 16, Lynde Point Light

Bock, Margaret. Genealogical material and miscellaneous clippings; also e-mail correspondence, 2003–2004.

———. "Lighthouse Memories." *Keeper's Log*, Summer 1994.

Bushy, Margaret. "Old Lighthouse Has Special Significance for Clinton Resident." *New Haven Register*, Nov. 21, 1975.

Naugatuck Daily News. "A Perilous Position," Apr. 18, 1901.

Neville, Scott. "To the Lighthouse." *Pictorial Gazette*, Nov. 29, 2003.

New Haven Register. "Lighthouse Work Begun in Fenwick," Mar. 24, 1940.

Chapter 17, Saybrook Breakwater Light

Berenson, Ron. "Lighthouse-Born Native Recalls Life on Sound." Newspaper clipping, date and source unknown.

Bock, Margaret. Genealogical material and miscellaneous clippings; also e-mail correspondence, 2003–2004.

———. "Lighthouse Memories." *Keeper's Log*, Summer 1994.Girodano, Alice. "Storied Lighthouse Goes Dark on Tourists." *Boston Globe*, Dec. 27, 1998.

New York Times. "A Lighthouse Keeper's Story," May 17, 1896.

Soundings. "Connecticut's 'License Plate Light' Gets a Badly Needed Sprucing Up," Nov. 1996.

Chapter 18, New London Harbor Light

Hamilton, Robert. "Crew from N.J. Cutter Is Sprucing Up the NL Harbor Light." *New London Day*, May 1, 2002.

Hewitt, Arthur. "Signals of the Sea." *Outlook*, Nov. 1904.

New London Day, "New London Harbor Light Is Fourth Oldest in Service; Light Supplies Big Industry," May 14, 1930.

"New London Harbor Lighthouse, Built in 1761, Fourth Lighthouse to Be Built in the United States." *Lighthouse Service Bulletin* 5, no. 41 (1939), pp. 178–180.

Wojtas, Joe. "Follow the Beam." *New York Times*, Nov. 3, 2002.

Chapter 19, New London Ledge Light

Bass, Elissa. "State Approves $100,000 Grant for Repairs to NL's Ledge Light." *New London Day*, Feb. 28, 1989.

Collins, David. "Automation May Close an Unusual Home at Sea." *New London Day*, Apr. 30, 1984.

Department of Commerce and Labor, description of New London Ledge Light Station, 1913. Record Group 26, 1082-13-5-2, National Archives.

Hartford Courant. "Visit Lovelorn Ernie's Lighthouse Haunts," Aug. 13, 1998.

Kimball, Carol W. "Building of New London Ledge Lighthouse." *New London Day*, May 5, 1988.

"The Lady of the Ledge," brochure from the New London Ledge Lighthouse Foundation, 2005.

"Light and Fog Signal, Black Ledge, New London Harbor, Connecticut." Report to the House of Representatives, 58th Congress, 2d session, Mar. 29, 1904.

Loveridge, G. Y. "They Keep the Light." *Providence Sunday Journal*, Dec. 9, 1951.

Manning, Edward H. "New London Ledge Lighthouse. Locally Known as Southwest Ledge Lighthouse. Some Notes on Its Construction and History." Typescript, New London Public Library, 1984.

New London Day. "How New Southwest Ledge Light Station Will Appear," Feb. 19, 1909.

———. "Southwest Ledge Light Is a Big Improvement," November 11, 1909.

Norman, Michael. "One Mile from the Frenzies of the World." *New York Times*, June 7, 1984.

O'Neill, Laurie A. "Keepers of the Light: A Pleasant Duty." *New York Times*, Aug. 9, 1981.

Thomson, William O. *Lighthouse Legends and Hauntings*. Kennebunk, ME: Scapes Me, 1998.

Tuttle, Roberta. "Ernie Comes to Call." *New London Day*, Nov. 10, 1985.

Chapter 20, Avery Point Light

Alcedo, Gladys. "Historic Lighthouse's Lantern Room to Get New Lease on Life." *New London Day*, June 27, 2003.

———. "Lighthouse Liftoff." *New London Day*, Dec. 5, 2001.

———. "Simmons to Announce Grant for Lighthouse." *New London Day*, Nov. 2, 2003.

Avery Point Lighthouse Society, http://apls.tripod.com.

Fisher, Sherry. "Avery Point Lighthouse Placed on Historic Register." *Advance*, Oct. 21, 2002.

Harrison, Tim. "Avery Point Added to Doomsday List." *Lighthouse Digest*, Dec. 1997.

Kimball, Carol W. "Avery Point Light Latecomer but It Deserves Preservation," *New London Day*, Sept. 21, 2000.

New London Day. "Dim Light," July 4, 1997.

———. "Group Asks Town to Help in Effort to Fix Up Lighthouse," Mar. 27, 2000.
Stamford Advocate. "Lantern Room from Avery Point Lighthouse to Be Rebuilt," June 27, 2003.
Streeter, James. "Avery Point Lighthouse Needs Your Help!" *Just for Seniors*, Aug. 2003.
Wesolowski, Jim. "A Christmas Light to Steer By." *Mystic River Press*, Dec. 18, 2003.

Chapter 21, Morgan Point Light

Arellano, Christopher. "Back on Top." *New London Day*, 1993 [exact date unknown].
Boehlert, Bart. "Christmas Light." *Coastal Living*, Nov./Dec. 1999.
Hartford Courant. "Family Restores Noank Lighthouse; Now Their Home Is a Beacon," May 15, 1993.
MacDonnell, Bob. "They're Right at Home in a Lighthouse," *Hartford Courant*, Aug. 13, 1999.
Maurer, David. "A Shore Thing." *Colonial Homes*, Aug. 1995.
New London Day. "Crook's Beacon Lighted by Gas," Aug. 8, 1921.
———. "New Light Great Aid to Mariners," Aug. 16, 1921.
———. "Noank's Light Keepers," July 20, 1899.
———. "Retires After 48 Years as Keeper of Light at Noank," Apr. 14, 1919.

Chapter 22, Stonington Harbor Light

D'Entremont, Jeremy. "Louise Pittaway: Keeper of Stonington's Lighthouse and Legacy." *Lighthouse Digest*, May 2004.
Historical Footnotes, bulletin of the Stonington Historical Society. Various issues, 1969–1995.
"Stonington Harbor, Connecticut." *Lighthouse Service Bulletin*, Vol. III, No. 67, July 1, 1929, pp. 296-297.
Tidings. "Rainy Day Ramblings," July 1986.

Chapter 23, Miscellaneous Lights and Lightships

Kiebish, Joe. "Two Lights on the River." *Lighthouse Digest*, Aug. 1998.
Lighthouse Digest. "Information Wanted: Chester Rock Lighthouse," May 1998.
New Haven Evening Register. "Harbor Men at Funeral of Tom Wilson," Sept. 30, 1910.
———. "Wilson Dies Lighting Long Wharf Beacon," Sept. 27, 1910.
Night Beacon, www.nightbeacon.com.
U.S. Coast Guard Historian's Office, www.uscg.mil/hq/g-cp/history/collect.html.
U.S. Coast Guard Lightship Sailors Association, www.uscglightshipsailors.org.

INDEX